DEVELOPING A LEARNING CULTURE IN NONPROFIT ORGANIZATIONS

DEVELOPING A LEARNING CULTURE IN NONPROFIT ORGANIZATIONS

STEPHEN J. GILL
Independent Consultant

Los Angeles | London | New Delhi
Singapore | Washington DC

For information:

SAGE Publications, Inc.
2455 Teller Road
Thousand Oaks, California 91320
E-mail: order@sagepub.com

SAGE Publications Ltd.
1 Oliver's Yard
55 City Road
London EC1Y 1SP
United Kingdom

SAGE Publications India Pvt. Ltd.
B 1/I 1 Mohan Cooperative
    Industrial Area
Mathura Road, New Delhi 110 044
India

SAGE Publications Asia-Pacific
    Pte. Ltd.
33 Pekin Street #02-01
Far East Square
Singapore 048763

Printed in the United States of America

Library of Congress Cataloging-in-Publication Data

Gill, Stephen J., 1947-
Developing a learning culture in nonprofit organizations / Stephen J. Gill.
    p. cm.
Includes bibliographical references and index.
ISBN 978-1-4129-6766-2 (cloth : acid-free paper)
ISBN 978-1-4129-6767-9 (pbk. : acid-free paper)
    1. Organizational learning—United States. 2. Community organization—United States. 3. Nonprofit organizations—United States. 4. Volunteers—United States. I. Title.

HD58.82.G52 2009
658.3'124—dc22   2008049619

This book is printed on acid-free paper.

09   10   11   12   13   10 9 8 7 6 5 4 3 2 1

Acquisitions Editor:	Kassie Graves
Editorial Assistant:	Veronica Novak
Production Editor:	Catherine M. Chilton
Copy Editor:	Liann Lech
Typesetter:	C&M Digitals (P) Ltd.
Proofreader:	Doris Hus
Indexer:	Diggs Publication Services
Cover Designer:	Gail Buschman
Marketing Manager:	Carmel Schrire

Contents

Foreword

Adaptation has always been a key to organizational survival, but never more so than today. That's why this is a much-needed book. Nonprofits are faced with funding uncertainty, altered expectations from consumers, complex and often competing regulations, and changing perceptions of how services should be provided and to whom.

It's an environment in which knowing what to do and how to do it requires a continuous process of learning that supports agency capacity development and performance improvement. Steve Gill has integrated theories about organizational culture and learning with reflections on cutting-edge practice—some from his own experience—to create a readable and hands-on guide for managers, board members, and practitioners.

Taking an open systems approach, he demonstrates the relationships between individual, team, whole organization, and community learning. Chapters provide both practice examples and application tools. Gill writes in a straight-from-the-shoulder (I've been there!) style that will be equally attractive to both students and practitioners.

This is one of a number of books that SAGE will be publishing over the next few years on the application of validated social science to social agency and nonprofit management and practice.

—Armand Lauffer
Professor Emeritus, University of Michigan
Co-chair, Sage Publications Editorial Board for the Human Services

Preface

The purpose of this book is to help you build a learning culture in your nonprofit organization. A learning culture will result in a high-performance, sustainable organization. The method for developing this kind of culture is evaluation, not in the traditional sense of a separate project designed to comply with program accountability expectations of funders and boards but rather continuous individual, team, organization, and community feedback and reflection that results in organizational learning and change.

New pressures on nonprofits are making organizational learning critical to their success and sustainability. Organizational learning means knowing how to know; knowing what you know; and knowing how to apply that knowledge to individual, team, organization, and community improvement. Whether large or small; human services, arts, or advocacy; well funded or hand-to-mouth—all nonprofits must be continually improving themselves. Organizational learning is the key to continuous improvement.

A hospital that uses the collective experience of its employees and customers to develop an effective way to conduct organization-wide strategic planning that then becomes the standard way for all departments to do their long-range planning is applying organizational learning. The hospital is learning from its own experience. A social services agency that evaluates each grant-funded program and uses this information to make incremental change, program by program, is not applying organizational learning. The agency might be improving programs, but it is not making systemic change that will improve the effectiveness of the organization over the long term.

Nonprofits are being called upon to demonstrate organizational learning to others. Stakeholders want to know that a nonprofit can operate effectively and efficiently and will achieve its stated goals. Having a noble mission is not enough anymore. Being a wise steward of resources and demonstrating results are paramount. Funders want to know that their money is being used wisely. Communities want to know that the nonprofit is contributing to improving the quality of life. Legislators want to know that the nonprofit status of these organizations is not being abused. The focus is shifting from outputs of each nonprofit program to sustained, organizational effectiveness.

Learning in nonprofits is not a new concept. To some extent, all nonprofits learn from their programs. Usually, this takes the form of spontaneous and unstructured conversations. Staff will talk among themselves about the success of a program, what they can do immediately to improve the program, and how they can deliver the program better the next time. However, this kind of program-focused critique is insufficient to build an effective organization.

A learning culture exists when an organization makes reflection, feedback, and sharing of knowledge part of the way it functions on a day-to-day basis. A nonprofit or non-governmental organization (NGO) that has a learning culture is continuously learning from its own experience, which means it has the capacity for improvement and success. In this way, a culture of learning contributes to the overall capacity of the organization.

Three major themes are driving current performance demands on nonprofits: the critical importance of nonprofits to a civil society; the growing size of the sector and its contribution to the economy; and the notoriety that has come from media coverage of financial and ethical problems in a few large, prominent nonprofits in the United States. Each of these themes makes a learning culture essential. The inconspicuous nonprofit, content with stable funding, stable staff, and fixed goals, is a thing of the past.

The purpose of this book is to provide practical ideas and tools for nonprofit leaders (managers, board members, volunteers, and consultants) to use in building a learning culture in their organizations. The target audience includes 501(c)(3) organizations and NGOs managed by a group of three or more people, with a board of trustees, regardless of its mission. Also, government agencies and civic organizations will benefit from the ideas and tools. One- or two-person organizations will find these ideas and tools difficult to implement, but they will still find something of value in the pages of this book.

In this book, I explain the importance of creating a culture of learning. I address this need in a wide range of organizations. I give examples of how an intentional focus on learning has helped non-profit organizations build their capacity and achieve their goals. I offer tools for helping managers facilitate learning at the individual, team, whole organization, and community levels.

The literature and the teaching about nonprofits (and for-profit organizations, for that matter) separate management, program evaluation, and training. Management is discussed in terms of leadership, supervision, and finances. Program evaluation emphasizes improving and assessing the worth and merit of a particular program within an agency. Workplace learning is usually talked about in terms of preservice; in-service; or formal, instructor-led training programs. This book argues for the integration of all three processes. Also included are models, specifically logic models and balanced scorecards, to be used as tools for learning. In addition, I describe how knowledge management and the physical workplace are critical elements of organizational learning.

Nonprofits do not need a great deal of time and money in order to learn. Examples are given of organizations that made learning a part of how they operate. Tools are provided for acquiring knowledge, skills, and attitudes as part of one's normal work and in collaboration with coworkers.

This book is for practitioners. It is intended to be a practical guide for using reflection and feedback to build the capacity for continuous learning in individuals, teams, whole organizations, and communities. Each chapter includes one or more tools that can be used for learning in your organization.

This is not an operations manual, nor is it an exhaustive resource. I have tried to provide enough information to help you identify potentially useful learning methods for your nonprofit. If something sounds like it might have a useful application in your organization, read more about it in the references. If you can, talk to people who have implemented an organizational learning approach in their own organizations. Then, work with a team of employees and volunteers in your organization who can help you adapt the methods to your particular circumstances. Try it out in a small way first, evaluate the results, and make changes. Finally, if it is effective, introduce the method to your whole organization. This is how organizations begin to learn.

Organization of This Book

The book starts by exploring the meaning of organizational learning and a learning culture. Then, each of the four levels of learning is described. Finally, the book addresses specific ways in which models and systematic evaluation can be used to enhance organizational learning.

Chapters

1. Need for a Learning Culture

This chapter explains what is meant by *learning culture*, contrasting it with employee training programs and organizational development. I explain why it is critical to develop this kind of culture in nonprofit organizations and why a culture of learning is necessary for organizational capacity building. I give examples of a variety of nonprofits that have developed this kind of culture.

2. Barriers to a Learning Culture

This chapter addresses the factors that can be impediments to developing a learning culture in any organization. Nonprofit leaders should be prepared for different kinds of resistance to changing their organization's culture. This chapter talks about this resistance and how to overcome the inevitable push-back from individuals, teams, whole organizations, and communities.

3. Developing a Learning Culture

This chapter describes the elements that go into developing a learning culture in any nonprofit. I explain how staff and volunteers contribute to this culture and how characteristics of the organization as a whole contribute to this culture.

4. Individual Learning

The focus of this chapter is the foundation of a learning culture: individuals acquiring new knowledge, skills, attitudes, and beliefs and applying this learning to improving performance. I explain how individuals can learn in organizations so that this learning contributes to organizational success, not simply their own development. I give examples of methods for individual learning that have led to nonprofit capacity building. I describe how individual learning becomes the building blocks for team, whole organization, and community learning.

5. Team Learning

This chapter makes the case for teams and team learning in nonprofits. I make the distinction between teams and work groups and explain how group learning creates well-functioning teams. I give examples of teams within nonprofits that contribute to organizational learning.

6. Whole Organization Learning

This chapter explains how whole organizations can learn collectively. I talk about key conditions for whole organization learning to occur. This builds on individual learning and team learning. I give examples of how whole organization learning in nonprofits leads to organizational success.

7. Community Learning

Communities can be defined by geography, membership, or constituency. Regardless of the kind of community, nonprofits have a responsibility to develop a culture of learning that will help these communities achieve their goals. This chapter gives examples of how, through organizational learning, nonprofits have contributed to enhancing the quality of life in their communities.

8. Learning From Evaluation

Organizational evaluation is critical for learning and developing a learning culture. The purpose of this chapter is to explain how nonprofits can use systematic evaluation to develop this culture. The intent is to be very practical and realistic within the context in which most nonprofits operate every day. This chapter also explains the importance of knowledge management in making maximum use of evaluative information.

9. Using Models to Learn

Nonprofits can learn from models. Logic models and balanced scorecards are two kinds of models that have been used effectively for this purpose. This chapter takes the reader through the process of using models. The reader sees how to use logic models and balanced scorecards to help an organization align itself for achieving results. Examples from large and small nonprofits are presented.

10. Summary

This chapter reemphasizes the link between learning and culture change. It reviews the four levels of organizational learning, and it reminds readers of the ways to develop a learning culture: through active use of evaluation. An organizational maturity model for nonprofits is offered as a tool for assessing where your organization is in terms of developing a learning culture.

Acknowledgments

This book is a result of the combined wisdom of many people whom I have had the pleasure of knowing and from whom I have learned much throughout my career. Some of these people are cited in the text and some have influenced my thinking through conversations and shared work experiences. I am especially indebted to John Baldoni, Theresa Behrens, Ben Benson, Jesse Bernstein, Roger Blair, Rob Brinkerhoff, Janet Callaway, Gwen Day, Leonard Gingerella, Rick Heydinger, Theo Jolosky, Cynthia Koch, Mark Lelle, Martha Legare, Tom Lehman, Bob Long, John Martin, Tom McGrath, Allen Menlo, Ricardo Millett, Joan Moore, Giovanna Morchio, Mim Munzel, Marylen Oberman, Joel Orosz, Rob Pasick, Frank Petrock, Molly Resnik, Julie Schumaker, Laurence Smith, Ed Surovell, Bill Svrluga, Iva Wilson, and Kathy Zurcher. I thank them for sharing their knowledge and insights with me regarding organizations and learning.

My thinking about organizational learning has also been influenced greatly by my HEC Group colleagues and our monthly dialogue. These comrades in mutual inquiry include Al Chambers, Judy Hallas, John Seeley, Leslie Stambaugh, Jim Stilwell, and Zena Zumeta.

I am very appreciative of the support for this book that I received from SAGE Publications. Kassie Graves and Armand Lauffer understood my vision for the book and made many helpful suggestions. John Tropman provided a valuable critique of the manuscript.

Of course, I could not have written this book without the patience and support of Nan Gill, who has been my wife, friend, business partner, colleague, and co-learner for nearly 39 years.

Stephen J. Gill
February 2009

SAGE Publications would like to thank the following reviewers: John Erlich, California State University, Sacramento; Robert L. Watson, Missouri State University; Diane DePanfilis, University of Maryland; Oren M. Levin-Waldman, Metropolitan College of New York; Armand Lauffer, University of Michigan (Emeritus).

1

Need for a Learning Culture

If you continue to do things the way you've been doing them, you'll continue to get the results you've been getting.

—Author Unknown

Need for Change

Expectations for the performance of nonprofits are increasing dramatically. Nonprofits are being held accountable for, at the same time, solving all the ills of our society, showing measurable results, and being financially solvent. Politicians, funders, boards of trustees, clients, and nonprofit managers are all demanding more from these organizations.

The increased attention on the sector is inevitable. Nonprofit organizations have become key players in the social and economic development of communities. Nonprofits fill service gaps that are not being addressed by local government and private business. Nonprofits form the backbone for the development of any community's social capital, and they make a significant, direct contribution to quality of life. In many communities, a nonprofit organization is the largest employer.

Nonprofits are critical to the maintenance of a democratic society. According to the Peter F. Drucker Foundation for Nonprofit Management, a healthy society requires three vital sectors: a public

1

sector of effective governments, a private sector of effective businesses, and a social sector of effective community organizations. This last group is the primary focus of this book, with government being secondary.

Lester Salamon and his associates at the Center for Civil Society Studies, which is part of the Johns Hopkins University Institute for Policy Studies, have concluded that the nonprofit sector is "a major economic force" around the world (Salamon, 1992). As recipients of more than $200 billion in charitable giving in the United States, the nonprofit sector accounts for 5% to 10% of the nation's economy (O'Neill, 2002). More than 1.1 million nonprofits (charities and private foundations) were registered with the U.S. government in 2007, a 4% increase over 2006 (Chronicle of Philanthropy, 2008). We can only conclude that the health of nonprofit organizations and their effectiveness in building the social capital of our communities is of vital interest to our nation and the world.

The rapid increase in size and economic impact of the nonprofit sector in the United States means that there will be greater demand for accountability. O'Neill (2002) writes in *Nonprofit Nation*:

> The new size of the nonprofit sector—11 million employees, $1 trillion in revenue, 1.8 million organizations—makes it inevitable that there will be more scandals, more negative press coverage, and more political attention. These developments will likely lead to more government oversight and regulation. How extensive and hostile this will be probably depends greatly on nonprofits' ability to work with government to make these changes as palatable as possible. (p. 247)

Negative articles by the media have created interest in nonprofit management reform like never before. According to Paul Light (2000),

> The nonprofit sector has never been under greater stress, as evidenced by doubts about its performance and ethical conduct. Federal budget cuts and private competition have affected already thin operating margins, while the highly publicized United Way and Salt Lake City Olympics scandals have sparked a broad debate about the effectiveness and legitimacy of nonprofit organizations. (p. 11)

He goes on to say,

> Despite all the warnings about reform, the pressure to get better is unlikely to abate and the number of reform efforts is unlikely to decline. To the contrary, the reform pressure seems to be increasing for the nonprofit sector. All the pieces are in place: growing demand from funders, rising expectations from clients, increased pressure from advocates both inside the sector and outside, burgeoning competition from other providers also both inside and outside the sector, and an apparent explosion in the number of organizational consultants ready to help the nonprofit sector identify problems and implement solutions. (p. 16)

The pressure from funders is especially acute. Foundations are looking for ways to ensure that their money is being invested wisely in these nonprofits. Foundations desire to make better decisions about where the money goes and want greater accountability for how the recipient uses the money. These philanthropies want to know that even if they are taking a risk on a new social venture, that grantee is managing the money well. The United Way of America's promotion of outcomes measures, the formation of Grantmakers for Effective Organizations, the W. K. Kellogg Foundation's Building Bridges programming effort, and articles on nonprofit management appearing in business journals such as *Harvard Business Review* are all evidence of this intensifying interest.

Prompted in part by a few of the more notorious scandals and by the amount of money that is controlled by a few very large nonprofit organizations, the media have taken special notice of what is happening in the sector. *Harvard Business Review* has published articles that put a microscope on private foundations and 501(c)(3) organizations (Bradley, Jansen, & Silverman, 2003; Porter & Kramer, 1999). The *Washington Post* ran a series of articles examining the Nature Conservancy's practices related to for-profit ventures (Stephens & Ottaway, 2003). Even *Fast Company* magazine has covered management practices at some of the most successful nonprofits (Hammonds, 2003) and has brought attention to an effort to track the financial performance of U.S. nonprofits by using data from the Internal Revenue Service's 990 tax filing form (Overholt, 2003).

At the same time that nonprofits are coming under greater scrutiny, they are being put under more pressure to plug gaps in the life of our communities. Stakeholders are expecting more from nonprofits and being vocal about it.

- Nonprofit board members want to feel confident that things are being done right and that they are not going to be embarrassed in the press.
- Nonprofit staff and volunteers want to be part of a well-functioning organization that provides needed services, is respected in the community, and will be around for a long time.
- Customers of nonprofits want responsive, timely services, and they want their needs met.
- Private donors want confidence that they have invested their money in a worthwhile and trustworthy organization.
- Foundations want to know that their money is being managed well, is being used for the purposes intended, and is making a difference.
- Legislators want to know that the tax-exempt status of nonprofits is not being abused.

Change does not come easy for nonprofits. Unlike for-profit businesses, nonprofits are driven by a social and educational mission, tax exempt because of this mission, accountable to the wider community, reliant on fundraising, dependent on volunteers (including board members), and staffed by people who are motivated heavily by intrinsic rewards. This combination of factors has made organizational effectiveness subordinate to providing services. Whether their missions are delivering health care, feeding the homeless, protecting the environment, representing a profession, staging theatrical events, or raising funds for cancer research, mission comes first, and often at the expense of long-term effectiveness and sustainability. Their very reason for being is to contribute to the public good in some significant way. That's the primary reason why people work for and volunteer with nonprofits. Understandably, developing an organization that has the capability to learn and change over time has not been a priority for nonprofits.

However, nonprofits can no longer put organizational learning on the back burner. The demand for change is too hot. They risk further government regulation, loss of funding, difficulty attracting competent employees, unwillingness of community leaders to serve on their boards, and dissatisfied customers.

Cultural Transformation

The response to this pressure on nonprofits to transform themselves shouldn't be piecemeal and bureaucratic; that will result only in temporary fixes that are not sustainable. Significant, sustained change will be born only out of a culture of learning. Like a petrie dish that provides a rich environment for microorganism growth, nonprofits that have a culture of learning are creating the conditions for growing their capacity to achieve maximum performance. They are continually growing, adapting, and becoming stronger. Learning and change is not only in response to outside stimulus, it is in their organizational DNA.

Schein (1985) has defined organizational culture as the values, basic assumptions, beliefs, expected behaviors, and norms of an organization; the aspects of an organization that affect how people think, feel, and act. Members of an organization have a shared sense of culture. A culture operates mostly unconsciously, manifested in every aspect of organizational life in subtle and not-so-subtle ways. From the rituals of celebration to how decisions are made, organizational culture is the artifacts and actions of members. Culture is passed on to new employees by what they are told and what they observe in the behavior, symbols, and documents around them.

A culture of learning is an environment that supports and encourages the collective discovery, sharing, and application of knowledge. In this kind of culture, learning is manifested in every aspect of organizational life. Staff and volunteers are continuously developing new knowledge together and applying collective knowledge to problems and needs.

In his definition of the kind of learning that helps people and organizations deal with the "permanent white water" faced by organizations today, Vaill (1996) talks about three kinds of learning: know-how (developing the skill to do something), know-what (understanding a subject), and know-why (seeing the meaning and value of something). A learning culture supports all three. Staff and volunteers are constantly learning new skills and improving old skills; increasing their understanding of mission, operations, and service to communities; and finding meaning and value in the mission, goals, and activities of the organization.

Organizational Learning

The kind of learning that results in organizational capacity building has been labeled organizational learning (Kim, 1993b). Organizational learning is the process of forming and applying collective knowledge to problems and needs. It is learning that helps the organization continually improve, achieve goals, and attain new possibilities. It is learning that taps into employee aspirations, fueling commitment and creating the energy to change.

An organization is learning when people are continuously creating, organizing, storing, retrieving, interpreting, and applying information. This information becomes knowledge (and, hopefully, wisdom) about improving the work environment; improving performance; improving operational (e.g., accounting, administration, communications) processes; and achieving long-range goals that will make the organization successful. The learning is intentional; it is for the purpose of increasing organizational effectiveness.

When an organization is learning, and not just individual members becoming more knowledgeable or more skilled, the dynamic interrelationship of its various parts contributes to the organization as a whole constantly becoming smarter about its effectiveness. It is creating an infrastructure that supports achieving the mission and attaining financial sustainability.

This infrastructure might be enhanced by an individual's participation in training programs, degree programs, certification, and other forms of education. However, unless the organization as a whole becomes stronger because of this learning, these kinds of individual activities are not organizational learning. The danger in thinking that smarter people make for a smarter organization is to assume that your organization is prepared when it isn't. For example, just because one or more managers in your nonprofit know about fundraising does not mean that the organization is maximizing its capability to raise money. Does your organization have a consciousness about fundraising that permeates everything you do? Are you continually trying to learn from successes and failures to become more effective? Have you learned how to put processes in place to support ongoing donor development? If your staff members do not understand their relationships to donors and you don't have a process for assessing these relationships, then your organization may not yet have the capacity it needs to succeed financially over the long term.

Researchers at the Urban Institute's Center on Nonprofits and Philanthropy have studied capacity building in nonprofits and have concluded that effective and sustainable organizations have:

1. Clear vision and mission that provide direction to the staff

2. Leadership that is continually being nurtured and developed

3. Resources that are used efficiently and creatively

4. Outreach that builds connections in the community and promotes a positive image

5. Products and services that are high quality ("How Are We Doing?" 2000)

Urban Institute is saying that all five of these conditions must exist for an organization to be effective and sustainable. Absent from this list are the usual demands: more money, more time, and more people. Although more resources might help a nonprofit develop some of these qualities, for most organizations, they need to learn how to use what they have more effectively. That is what will make them effective and sustainable over the long run.

Examples of Organizational Learning

Organizational learning can look different in different kinds of nonprofits. Here are some examples.

Community-Based Service Agency

A start-up management support organization (MSO) for nonprofits has the mission of helping a Midwestern county's nonprofits achieve their missions through effective management. This newly formed resource for other nonprofits is trying to become a model of capacity building in the community. To do this, the staff have had to take enormous risks in offering training, consulting, technical assistance, and information management. The process of taking these risks and experimenting with new programs has given the staff a better understanding of the needs of the community and how they have to change their own organization to better serve those needs.

This MSO convened a group of community leaders that was then asked periodically for advice about what staff should be doing to be successful as an organization. The MSO staff hired an evaluator, during their start-up phase, to serve as a mirror for the organization. They met with this person monthly to discuss their progress. The evaluator's role was to continually ask questions such as

- What are your goals?
- What will indicate success to you?
- How will your current programs and services help you achieve the outcomes and impact that you want?
- What should you continue doing, and what should you change in order to be successful?

The process they used of experimentation, reflection, and learning has become integral to the way this nonprofit operates.

Community-Based Arts Organization

An arts organization provides a wide variety of performing arts for all ages, works with schools on arts education, and is a center for performing arts in its region. Its board of directors has been building its capacity for planning and getting results. They have learned how to use an ongoing board planning process created by Mark Light, called Results Now™, to address four key questions:

1. Where do we want this organization to go tomorrow?

2. Who needs to do what so that we can get there?

3. What must get done today?

4. Are we on track to get the results we want?

The board of this arts organization has developed a process that keeps board members and management focused on the most important goals and also allows the flexibility to take advantage of new opportunities. In 10 years, subscribers grew from 3,500 to 27,000, its audience base grew from 22,000 to 300,000 people, revenues grew from $500,000 to $10 million, and sponsorships grew from $20,000 to $1.1 million. Although it is clear that they have achieved great success, they continually re-examine their direction, their activities, and how they are organized to manage this growth and achieve results in the future. Strategic planning is ingrained in the life of the organization.

Large Research Hospital

The nursing service of a nonprofit, university-affiliated hospital underwent a whole-organization change effort, the purpose of which was to reframe the role of nursing in the hospital system. The seminal event for employees was a meeting that brought all of the staff together in one place. This voluntary event included not only the nurses, but also a variety of stakeholders, including physicians, School of Nursing faculty, and patients. It was the result of 8 months of planning by an active, 30-person planning team. Taking this amount of time and building a large and diverse team were essential in building a sense of ownership in the process and the results and in preparing the organization as a whole for what would be profound changes initiated by the event.

It helped that the director of nursing was very committed to what was being done. She presented her vision and made a case for that vision based on data from an environmental scan. This triggered a process of organizational self-examination and reflection. Participants added to the director's vision, and a planning team shaped what resulted into a new vision statement for nursing. The director then presented this statement to the whole planning team and had participants validate the new vision.

In each of these examples of organizational learning, staff learned how to learn about their organizations and how to bring about needed change. Now they know how to bring about organizational improvement in a way that they didn't know before these interventions. None of these organizations can afford to stand still. Whether they serve other nonprofits, art patrons, or hospital patients, the world around them is changing, and these organizations must continually build their capacity to learn and improve or they will rapidly become irrelevant. Each has developed a culture that supports learning and change.

Sources of Pressure
for Organizational Improvement

A learning culture is created when organizational learning is ingrained in the day-to-day habits of the whole organization. This kind of culture is developed through an ongoing evaluation process of inquiry, feedback, reflection, and change. The remainder of this book explains how this process of evaluation contributes to a culture of learning and what can be done by nonprofits to create a culture that supports and sustains organizational learning.

Start by asking some key questions. What is the baseline? What is the gap between an organization's current effectiveness and how effective it wants to become?

Begin with an overall assessment of your organization. Following are two tools to assist you in this process. The first is the Sources of Pressure for Organizational Improvement (see Tool 1.1). This tool will help your organization identify internal and external pressures for learning and change, and it can be used to facilitate staff and volunteer input. Put the chart on something large that can be displayed in front of a group, such as flip-chart paper or a mural, or project it onto a screen. Invite employees, board members, other volunteers, and other stakeholders to participate in this activity.

Ask the group, "What pressures are you feeling for organizational improvement?" "How is the economy, government, etc., putting pressure on us?" Fill in the chart. Ask staff and board members to discuss these pressures. This is a good way to surface the concerns, fears, questions, challenges, and opportunities that are on everyone's minds. Ask them to first say, either individually or after small group discussions, which additional stakeholders should be on the chart. Then ask participants to say, either individually or after small group discussion, what the expectations are that each of these stakeholders has for learning in your nonprofit. What are their performance demands? What would indicate success to each of these groups? Insert these responses on the chart and discuss them with the whole group. Ask, "What are the implications of each of these expectations for the way our organization should operate?" The activity itself should take 60 to 90 minutes if the group is small (less than 12) and longer if the group is larger.

Collect these responses and report them back to all of the participants within the week following this activity. Use this summary as a springboard for planning initiatives to address the expectations of the various stakeholders.

| Tool 1.1 | Sources of Pressure for Organizational Improvement |

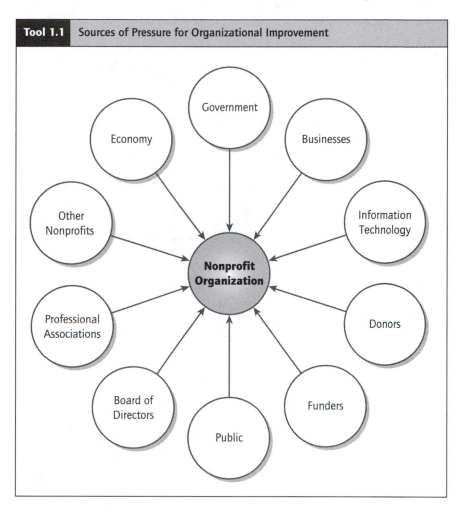

Organizational Self-Assessment

The second tool is a survey instrument for assessing the status of overall functioning of a nonprofit organization (see Tool 1.2). It is not enough to simply administer this instrument and collect the data. The real value is in using the data for organizational self-reflection and then acting on what is learned from that process. Before using this tool, work with your stakeholders on a plan for how the data will be used for this purpose. For example, you might analyze the difference in results among key groups, such as management, staff, volunteers

Tool 1.2 Organizational Self-Assessment

To what extent do you agree with each of the following statements? Please check one of the boxes following each statement. If you believe that you do not know enough about the organization to respond to the statement, check the "Don't Know" column.

	Strongly Agree	Agree	Neutral	Disagree	Strongly Disagree	Don't Know
This organization has a clear vision for the future.						
Employees and volunteers are committed to the mission of this organization.						
This organization is committed to continuous improvement.						
Leaders are continually being developed for future roles in this organization.						
This organization is always looking for ways to use resources more effectively and efficiently.						
Employees and volunteers would change this organization if it would help them to better meet the mission.						
The board pays attention to enhancing overall performance of the organization.						
This organization uses its own experience to learn how to perform more effectively.						
Evaluation is part of every program and operation of this organization.						

	Strongly Agree	Agree	Neutral	Disagree	Strongly Disagree	Don't Know
Evaluation results are used in organizational planning.						
Employees and volunteers receive appropriate orientation and training.						
Employees and volunteers are clear about the link between what they are doing and the strategic goals of the organization.						
Learning and improving permeates everything that this organization does.						
Individual employees and volunteers are engaged in action learning.						
Work teams are engaged in action learning.						
Effective leadership is recognized and rewarded.						
The organization works with the community for mutual learning.						
This organization is committed to building its capacity to be effective over the long term.						
The organization's products and services match what customers want.						
The resources (people, money, facilities, equipment, etc.) are aligned with intended outcomes of the organization.						

(including board members), community partners, and clients. Decide who will see the results of the assessment, how the results will be presented to them, in what format they will react to the findings, how their learning will be recorded, and how their recommendations will be advanced in the organization. Then follow through with the plan. One of the most frustrating and demoralizing situations for staff occurs when management conducts a survey, raising hopes for improvement, and then does nothing with the data.

The survey instrument addresses six areas of organizational learning, five from the Urban Institute research mentioned earlier and one addressing whole organization learning:

1. Clear vision and mission that provide direction to the staff

2. Leadership that is continually being nurtured and developed

3. Resources that are used efficiently and creatively

4. Outreach that builds connections in the community and promotes a positive image

5. Products and services that are high quality

6. Learning that continuously improves the whole organization

Summary

Nonprofits today need to be learning constantly. College degrees or occasional seminars and workshops are not enough anymore. The world of nonprofits is changing, and this change will only continue and probably become even more rapid. New funding requirements, new technologies, increasing demands for greater accountability, increasing expectations for the sector, and more intersectoral collaboration are all fueling change. The only way to build capacity to keep up and survive is by creating a culture that supports continuous learning at the individual, team, whole organization, and community levels of nonprofits. This learning is the acquisition and application of new knowledge, skills, and ways of working together that make the organization as a whole more effective. A learning culture is created by the way an organization is led, the style and frequency of communication, how incentives are linked to learning, and the design of the physical environment. The remainder of this book explains how to create and sustain this kind of culture.

2

Barriers to a Learning Culture

Telling the truth to people who may not want to hear it is, after all, the chief purpose of evaluation.

—Eleanor Chelimsky

Significant barriers stand in the way of learning in organizations. These barriers are manifested in subtle and not-so-subtle resistance to creating a culture of learning. If you want to be successful over the long term, you have no choice but to face these barriers and overcome them. Barriers to a learning culture are examined in some depth in this chapter:

- Program focus
- Limited resources
- Work-learning dichotomy
- Passive leadership
- Nonlearning culture
- Resistance to change
- Not discussing the undiscussable
- Need for control
- Focus on short-term, simple solutions
- Skilled incompetence
- Blame, not gain language

Program Focus

One barrier to developing a learning culture is that the attention of staff and volunteers is usually on program delivery, not organization improvement. As mission-driven organizations, nonprofits attract people who want to serve others. These staff and volunteers choose to participate in a nonprofit in large part to make a difference for the public good: education; the arts; health care; the environment; social services; or the mutual benefit of a group of people, such as a church or professional association. Their sights are on delivering programs that fulfill one or more of these purposes. Putting on programs is what gives people a sense of satisfaction in their work. Building a viable organization for the long term is not a primary motivator of staff and volunteers.

Being program focused is understandable given the mission of nonprofits, the way they are funded, and how they are led. Their missions are usually to address the pressing needs of society or to provide some kind of educational or artistic benefit to society. Staff and volunteers sign on because they are attracted to these missions, not because they aspire to be part of a learning culture. For example, if you were to tell the staff of a hospice that they will have to spend some time working on organizational effectiveness, their initial reaction will be disappointment that they won't be using this time for helping the terminally ill patients that they came to serve. We often see this phenomenon in board members who ignore evidence of failing leadership or ineffective organizational processes because they joined the board to participate in something positive. They did not join to deal with internal strife or management challenges.

A program focus is also a result of the way nonprofits are funded. Grants, endowment funds, and fees are usually designated for specific programs. For example, a youth service organization receives a grant from a foundation to put on a college-prep workshop for disadvantaged youth during the summer. The nonprofit is held accountable by the funder for delivering the workshop, not for the effectiveness of its organization. Funders might ask what happened in the workshop and who and how many people attended. Funders rarely give grants to answer questions such as, "How capable have you become as an organization to ensure the college success of disadvantaged youth?" The youth service organization is held accountable for delivering the program as specified, not for the agency learning how to continue to help clients achieve success. This is understandable; funders enjoy the role of supporting something new and different, and nonprofits do things that are new and different because that's what is being funded.

Another explanation for this program focus is that funding organizations are departmentalized, whether a government agency or foundation, and therefore, they tend to support departmentalized programs. For example, a foundation that has established college access as a priority funding area will have a department with responsibility for funding programs that give disadvantaged youth opportunities to prepare for and enroll in college. That department is not likely to fund improved performance of the organizations that manage those programs.

Limited Resources

Many nonprofits are existing "hand to mouth," with limited time and money for anything other than delivering core services. The money is spent as soon as it comes in the door. Whatever money is left after paying for staff time is used to secure more funding. This can be a roadblock when learning is equated with expensive external educational programs and consultants. Staff and volunteers may not be aware of the many opportunities for learning that do not require large expenditures of time and money. To them, learning has a cost that they do not think they can afford.

Work-Learning Dichotomy

Another barrier is the assumption that work and learning are different activities. A common belief is that learning is something that happens to individuals only in classrooms, at conferences, or at the occasional staff retreat. This is a mental model that prevents people from taking advantage of the many learning opportunities in their work.

Some people believe that attending workshops on fundraising, grant writing, legal liability, or volunteer management is all they need in order to be effective. However, these training programs do not necessarily ensure organizational learning. An orchestra can have the finest cellist, the finest pianist, the finest violinist, the finest trumpet player, and even the finest conductor and still fail to excite the audience. Having all of this talent in close proximity is no guarantee that they will learn how to produce beautiful music together, night after night; so, too, with nonprofit organizations. Having talented and committed individuals on your staff is only part of the equation. They must know how to work and learn together.

The assumption that learning is "extra" is another barrier to maximizing the potential for any organization to build its capacity at the individual, team, whole organization, and community levels. In fact, given the rapid pace of change and the enormous amounts of information being exchanged minute by minute, work and learning must be integrated. The executive director of a food bank, overwhelmed with the severity of the need, can't wait for a college degree program or even a single class to improve the collection and distribution of perishable foods. He or she has to stay informed about new technology and how to best organize people to take advantage of that technology. He or she must ask, "What do we have to do to reduce the time and cost to get food from where it is produced to the people who are hungry, and, at the same time, keep our staff and volunteers motivated?" This is learning that has to happen in the field and on the run.

Passive Leadership

Leadership can be another barrier to learning. Because board members want to be associated with successful programs, they often create, with the cooperation of staff, a conspiracy of silence about the organization's leaders. Staff will report successes because that's what they think board members want to hear. In response, board members don't ask tough questions about the organization. Staff and volunteers can become frustrated and disenchanted when they are faced with challenging organizational issues and may try to avoid them. This avoidance of issues has contributed to serious problems in major nonprofits in the past, resulting in mismanagement of funds, overly risky investments, ethical lapses, and outright theft.

As Ruth McCambridge, editor-in-chief of *The Nonprofit Quarterly,* writes,

> This sector is full of true believers. They bring energy and the sometimes single minded passion that drives change in society but some of the most painful missteps we have seen in this sector and the public policy pushed by it are the result of groups refusing to question their own most basic assumptions. This is excruciatingly human. (McCambridge, 2006, pp. 13–14)

Leaders are reluctant to ask the questions behind the questions. Is this is the right thing to be doing? Should we be separating abused and neglected children from their families? Should we be encouraging abused women to leave their husbands? Should we be building shelters for homeless people while not doing anything about low-income, permanent housing in the community? Should we be increasing ticket prices for our community orchestra while making the music less accessible to low-income residents? Each of these questions challenges underlying assumptions about the nonprofit. The culture in many nonprofits does not support this kind of self-questioning. Everyone assumes that everyone else thinks it is the right thing to be doing; it's the Abilene Paradox (Harvey, 1996). The Abilene Paradox occurs when members of a group are reluctant to voice what they perceive to be a contrary view for fear of being ostracized in some way. Each person's silence results in the group taking action that is not what would be consensus if everyone said what he or she actually believed. This is a common dilemma for nonprofit boards.

Nonlearning Culture

Current culture can be another barrier to learning. According to Schein (1985), organizational culture consists of the values, basic assumptions, beliefs, expected behaviors, and norms of an organization. These are the aspects of an organization that affect how people think, feel, and act. An organization that has a culture that, in effect, closes off communication as well as stifles honest feedback and reflection does not allow for organizational learning to occur. Some examples of this include the following:

- Employees passing around stories (true or not) about coworkers being forced out because they tried something new
- Managers telling subordinates to develop their skills but then chastising them for taking the time to attend a training event
- Rewarding employees for individual effort, but not for engaging in cross-functional team problem solving
- Supporting a study of the viability of a new service and then not using that study's findings and recommendations
- Surveying employees about their job satisfaction and customers about their satisfaction with services, and then not making any visible changes based on the results.

In some organizations, the culture discourages risk taking, but without risk taking, there is little opportunity for learning. People have to be willing to apply new knowledge and skills, even when not immediately supported by others. Consider, for example, a local Habitat for Humanity affiliate that received a request to build a home jointly sponsored by three religious institutions: Christian, Muslim, and Jewish. This would be a difficult decision for a Habitat affiliate at any time, but particularly challenging in a post-9/11 environment. The risk takers on the board said, "Let's try it, and let's learn from the experience." The board members who supported the status quo said, "That's not our mission. Our purpose is low-income housing. It's not our job to solve the ethnic divides in our community." Both sides have a point, but one position encourages learning and the other position is a barrier to learning. One side is willing to take risks and the other side is reluctant to put the organization's reputation on the line.

Resistance to Change

Resistance to change is the tendency we have to maintain the familiar and not take the risk of trying something new and different. For example, changing from a command-and-control style of leadership to an empowerment form of leadership; changing from an elaborate, hierarchical organizational structure to a flat, boundaryless organizational structure (Ashkenas, Ulrich, Jick, & Kerr, 1995); and changing from an individual-centered work process to a team-centered work process are difficult transitions because employees tend to approach the change in terms of how it will affect them personally.

Like people living under repressive regimes who fear democracy, many nonprofit organizations suffering from low employee morale, increasing debt to creditors, and limited impact on constituents would still rather stay with what they know than make a major change. They fear the unknown and worry that things could get worse. They also fear losing what they have. At least the known is a situation they understand and can control, and over which they have a level of power and influence. They naturally think, "What problems will this change cause for me?" rather than, "What can I learn from the change process that will build my capacity and the capacity of the organization?"

Not Discussing the Undiscussable

Not discussing the undiscussable prevents information from surfacing in your organization that could be very useful for learning and change (Argyris, 1990). All work groups and whole organizations have topics that they have implicitly agreed not to discuss. This is a shared but unspoken understanding that the issue will not be mentioned— the proverbial "elephant in the room." Your subordinates will not talk to you about their dissatisfaction with how much time you spend in the office. Your work group will not discuss problems with the reorganization plan that they have been working on for months but think is a waste of time and resources. Your coworkers will not confront each other with communication problems for fear of embarrassing someone and then having criticism come back at them. The people who have the information and the person who needs to hear the information are unknowingly colluding with each other. An unfortunately common form of this collusion is management withholding information (for example, finances) from staff who would benefit from knowing and staff not asking for greater transparency from management. This collusion prevents discussion of the very things that get in the way of organizational learning. Until attention is turned to the "elephant," there will be very little learning.

Need for Control

People have a need for control, and this gets acted out in the structures that they build for their organizations. Organizational charts, policy manuals, published rules and regulations, performance evaluation processes, budget and expenses monitoring, internal security systems, and the design of physical spaces are all means of directing, monitoring, and limiting the behavior of employees and volunteers. This has value when managing the complexity of a large nonprofit. The structural elements ensure that (a) people know where they fit in an organization; (b) practice and application are standardized; (c) everyone is on the same page concerning regulatory requirements, which minimizes liability for the organization; (d) there is a shared commitment toward continued quality improvement resulting from evaluation processes; (e) revenue and expenses are within projections and allow the organization to achieve its mission; and (f) space design makes the best use of physical space as well as ensures maximum functionality.

However, these elements can also have the effect of constraining the behavior of staff and volunteers to the point that learning is stifled. For example, an organizational chart, although helpful in letting people know where they fit, sets the expectation that communication and authority may only flow through certain predefined channels. This can prevent one staff member from communicating vital information to another staff member who is not within a particular line of authority. Silos of knowledge and skill are created in this way.

Focus on Short-Term, Simple Solutions

Focusing on short-term, simple solutions to complex problems might provide some relief in a difficult situation, but it does not help people learn. Removing a challenging employee from a team without confronting the problem that the employee is surfacing, reviewing all expenses submitted for reimbursement because you suspect padding of reimbursement requests without analyzing the reimbursement process, or using layoffs to reduce costs without examining the entire enterprise for other opportunities to control costs or increase revenue are all examples of actions that might be necessary but represent short-term, simple solutions to complex problems. These situations offer tremendous opportunities for learning for everyone in the organization. However, by taking the easy way out and not investing time, effort, resources, and emotion in the big picture and long view, there is temporary relief, but no one learns how to solve these kinds of problems.

Skilled Incompetence

Skilled incompetence is a strong label, but an accurate description Argyris (1990) has invented for a common operative disease of managers. This is our natural tendency to avoid embarrassing or threatening interactions with others by changing the subject, placing blame on others, or not accepting responsibility for problem situations. When you do this, you are missing an opportunity to learn from others and from reflecting on your own behavior. To learn, you must seek feedback from others. You must ask yourself, "What is it about what I am doing or saying that contributes to other people behaving in ineffective and destructive ways?" You will need feedback from others to answer this question, and you will have to listen non-defensively to the answers (Frydman, Wilson, & Wyer, 2000).

Blame, Not Gain Language

The language we commonly use with each other can also be a barrier to learning. In their book *Ending the Blame Culture* (Pearn, Mulrooney, & Payne, 1998), the authors give examples of the difference between an organization's language that is judgmental and punitive (blame) and language that facilitates learning (gain) (see Table 2.1).

The blaming language on the left side of this table is a barrier to learning. It immediately puts the other person on the defensive and stifles any interest that person might have had in receiving constructive feedback, reflecting on its meaning, and using what he or she has learned to improve the organization. On the other hand, "gain" language makes it more likely that the other person will be receptive to thinking about an experience in a constructive way. That person is likely to feel respected and understood, and therefore more willing to honestly examine events for what can be learned from the experience.

Table 2.1   Blame and Gain Language

Blame Behaviors	Gain Behaviors
Judging: "You were wrong."	Exploring: "What happened?"
Showing emotion: "I'm furious with you."	Remaining calm: "Try not to worry about it."
Reacting to what you think happened: "You should have . . ."	Finding out exactly what happened: "Let's take this one step at a time."
Blaming people for getting it wrong: "You should never have let this happen."	Focusing on the process that allowed the mistake to happen: "What could have been done differently?"
Finding fault: "You have only yourself to blame."	Providing support: "This must be difficult for you but don't forget this has happened to us all."
Focusing on effects: "This is going to cause enormous problems for me."	Focusing on causes: "What I want to focus on is all the things that enabled this to happen to us all."
Assuming the person should feel guilty/be contrite: "You really have only yourself to blame."	Assuming the person wants to learn: "What are the main lessons for us?"
Seeing mistakes as something that must be avoided: "This must never happen again."	Seeing mistakes as part of a learning process: "We can learn a lot from this."

SOURCE: Pearn, Mulrooney, and Payne (1998).

Summary

People have a natural tendency to build barriers to learning in organizations. Even the best-intentioned manager will create controls, ways of communicating, styles of leadership, and mental models that become roadblocks to sharing information, applying new knowledge, and discovering ways to work together effectively. The first step in lowering these barriers is awareness. Management, employees, and volunteers (including board members) should discuss these barriers openly and regularly.

Tool 2.1 is designed to help with this discussion. Work in groups of 6 to 12 people to identify specific examples of barriers

Tool 2.1	Barriers to Organizational Learning	
Barrier	*Example* What is a specific example in your organization of this barrier to learning?	*Overcome the Barrier* What can be done in your organization to overcome this barrier and achieve organizational learning?
Program Focus at the Exclusion of Organization Focus		
Limited Resources		
Work-Learning Dichotomy		
Passive Leadership		
Nonlearning Culture		
Resistance to Change		
Not Discussing the Undiscussable		
Need for Control		
Focus on Short-Term, Simple Solutions		
Skilled Incompetence		
Blame, Not Gain Language		

in your organization. For example, in what way does your organization keep the focus on programs rather than the organization as a whole? Discuss this in your group and then write in one example of this. Then talk about what the group could do differently to be more whole-organization focused and achieve greater organizational learning.

3

Creating a
Learning Culture

Imagination is the beginning of creation. You imagine what you desire, you will what you imagine and at last you create what you will.

—George Bernard Shaw

To create a culture in which learning is the rule, not the exception, nonprofits must remove the barriers to learning and reward behaviors that facilitate learning: risk taking, action learning, feedback, and reflection. For example, a nonprofit that provides mental health and substance abuse intervention services has created a program evaluation, research, and training arm. This new department examines the effectiveness of the organization's programs. In collaboration with a local university and external funding, the nonprofit has made learning from its own programs integral to the way it functions. New knowledge from the evaluation of its programs immediately becomes part of planning and staff training and then is disseminated to the mental health field.

Another example is a community foundation that believes it should always strive to do better for its customers, so it periodically asks grant applicants for feedback about the quality of the foundation's services. The foundation uses this information in staff meetings to take stock of its performance and identify changes it can make to increase customer satisfaction. They ask themselves questions such as "What can we do to streamline the application process?" "What can we do to help grant applicants prepare better applications?" and "What can we do to help nonprofits that we fund become more sustainable?"

Still another example is a management support organization that experiments with new training programs for local nonprofits. Feedback from these sessions and data from follow-up surveys are used to change the program content and change the way in which nonprofit managers and their board members are assisted in the community. Some programs are continuously improved, some are discontinued, and new programs are added over time.

In each of these examples, self-examination is central to the work of the organization. These organizations regularly assess themselves and then use that feedback to adjust and change their goals as well as their programs and processes.

Nonprofits must take the time to step back, take a look at themselves, make sure that what they are doing is aligned with what they want to achieve, and then have the courage to change if needed. In describing this kind of change, Sussman (2003) writes that

> high-performing nonprofit organizations, those demonstrating adaptive capacity, are voracious learners. They are inquisitive in that they seek out data and information: they use it to learn, and then they apply and share their newfound knowledge. (p. 22)

Often, the pressure for training and education in nonprofits comes in the wake of faddish reform efforts that start in other sectors. Paul Light (2000) points to the danger of hitching the nonprofit wagon to these movements. His concern is that reform is still just a short-term effort to address gaps in performance. Reform tends to homogenize organizations, whereas a learning culture promotes diversity in thought and action. Nonprofits don't need the latest business fad; they need a culture that supports continuous learning for continuous improvement.

Continuous Learning

In a learning culture, the acquisition of new knowledge and skills is supported by aspects of the organization's environment that encourage surfacing, noticing, gathering, sharing, and applying new knowledge. These conditions are not always readily visible or measurable, but they are always affecting organizational learning. The culture of the whole organization, the ways in which people communicate with each other, the ways in which people lead, how the organization evaluates its performance, the physical environment of workspaces, and knowledge management all have an impact on sustaining learning over time.

This is a culture of inquiry. It is an environment in which staff and volunteers feel safe to ask questions about the purpose and quality of what they are doing for customers and other stakeholders. Employees are empowered to ask questions such as the following:

What customer outcomes do we want to achieve?

Are we organized to achieve those outcomes?

Is this program helping customers achieve those outcomes?

What should we be doing differently to make it more likely that we will achieve those customer outcomes?

And even more fundamentally,

How can we continue to know our organizational effectiveness?

How can we use that information collectively to change and grow?

The role of nonprofit managers is to help shape a culture of learning; to make the pursuit of learning part of the fabric of organizational life. Learning should be apparent in the values and expected behaviors. Staff and volunteers should be expecting to acquire new knowledge and new skills, and to have their beliefs challenged on a day-to-day basis.

Role of the Board

Nonprofit board members are critical to creating a culture of learning because they set the tone for the entire organization. If they are practicing and modeling learning, it is likely the whole organization will follow.

One framework for engaging a board in learning is The Strategic Board™ model. This model promotes board member involvement in organizational learning. The model uses an approach to board and staff planning that helps board members and staff learn together and learn how to learn together (Light, 2001). At one level, it takes them through a joint process for creating four plans: (a) a leadership plan (vision, values, and goals); (b) a delegation plan (who does what); (c) a management plan (what needs to get done immediately); and (d) a vigilance plan (monitoring, evaluation, and accountability). At another level, the process teaches board members and staff how to work together for a common purpose and thus build their capacity to be an effective organization. Mark Light, developer of this model, used it with much success while president of several arts organizations and then with other types of nonprofits. It is an effective way of disrupting the usual patterns of passive participation and making board members active in helping the organization learn about itself.

Renz (2004) suggests that boards need to answer two central questions for themselves:

- What is the work this board needs to accomplish to meet the needs of this organization?
- How do we best connect this organization to the community and its most important constituencies?

By addressing these two questions, board members are learning what really matters to them as a group. The answers will fall along a continuum from a strong strategic focus to a strong operational focus and from broad and active stakeholder involvement in decisions to a few leaders making all of the decisions for the organization. Each nonprofit must decide for itself where its board should be on these two continua. The process engages a board in self-examination and reflection. The answers will not be the same for every board.

Organizational Learning

Organizational learning is defined as the process of forming and applying collective knowledge to problems and needs. It is learning that helps the organization continually improve, achieve goals, and attain new possibilities and capacities. It taps into employee aspirations, fueling commitment and creating the energy to change.

An organization learns when its employees are continuously creating, organizing, storing, retrieving, interpreting, and applying information. This information becomes knowledge (and, hopefully, wisdom) for improving the work environment, improving performance, improving work processes, and achieving long-range goals that will make the organization successful. The learning is intentional; it is for the benefit of the organization as a whole.

Organizational learning is not a simple process. It is constant reexamining and changing ideas about how to be effective. Organizational learning demands long-term work at changing the day-to-day behaviors and practices of individuals, groups, organizations, and communities. This kind of learning requires commitment and leadership.

Methods of learning can be directed at one or more of the four levels: individual learning, small group learning, whole organization learning, and community learning. This separation of levels is somewhat artificial because considerable overlap occurs among the levels. However, you will find that the categorization makes it easier to identify and select strategies that fit problems, challenges, and needs as they arise.

Furthermore, the complexity and rapid change of work today requires collective learning. Members of a work team learn how to solve problems together. A large nonprofit learns how to do strategic planning as a total organization. In neither of these examples do they simply complete the immediate task; rather, each develops the capacity to perform these tasks successfully in the future.

Learning is critical to the survival of organizations in these rapidly changing times. As Noer (1996) said,

Organizations of the future will not survive without becoming communities of learning. The learning organization is no academic fad or consultant's buzzword. It is absolutely essential for organizations to learn from their environments, to continually adjust to new and changing data, and, just as is the case with the individual, to learn how to learn from an uncertain and unpredictable future. (p. 176)

Garvin (1993) explains this need for a commitment to organizational learning in this way:

> Continuous improvement requires a commitment to learning. How, after all, can an organization improve without first learning something new? Solving a problem, introducing a product, and reengineering a process all require seeing the world in a new light and acting accordingly. In the absence of learning, [organizations]—and individuals—simply repeat old practices. Change remains cosmetic, and improvements are either fortuitous or short-lived. (pp. 78–79)

Garvin argues that organizations learn through five main activities: problem solving systematically, experimenting with new approaches, learning from their own experience and past history, learning from the experiences and best practices of others, and transferring knowledge quickly and efficiently throughout the organization. Nonprofits must find ways to build these activities into their daily lives. An organization that employs these activities is constantly looking for the root cause of problems, trying new ways to solve those problems, informing others about what was learned from these experiments, and using this learning to improve. This kind of nonprofit has developed a system for implementing these activities that works within the culture of that organization. A responsive and nimble local Boys and Girls Club can try things and do things in a way that is not possible for the national Boys and Girls Clubs of America to do. However, the larger and more bureaucratic organization can develop its own system for institutional change. One organization is learning how to make local communities better places for kids, and the other is learning how to respond effectively to the needs of its member clubs.

Senge (1990) explains that organizations learn by applying five disciplines. The first is *personal mastery,* which is personal capacity building. The second is *mental models,* which is challenging and changing our way of thinking about the world around us. The third is *shared vision,* which is achieving a collective sense of where we want to go as an organization and how to achieve that goal. The fourth is *team learning,* which is small groups of people learning how to learn together. And the fifth is *systems thinking,* which is recognition of the interdependence of the parts of a social system and how to leverage change throughout that system. Senge is asking us to change the way we typically think about learning. He is asking us to look at organizations as open systems that have a dynamic interdependence of people, resources, and structure that can be leveraged for positive change. People need to build their own capacity to learn and change, each team's capacity to learn and change, and the whole organization's capacity to learn and change.

As you can see from these definitions of organizational learning, simply attending classes, workshops, and seminars is not sufficient. These training events might contribute to individual learning, but they are not sufficient for long-term individual, team, and organization success. For that, nonprofits need to develop their own unique processes for assimilating new information, translating that information into knowledge, applying that knowledge to real needs, and receiving feedback to revise the information and reshape the knowledge.

Organizational learning is a continuous process, whereas training is an event that occurs at brief points in time. Learning from the serendipity as well as the design of work, followed by immediate application and feedback, can't happen in a classroom. Learning has to occur when and where there is opportunity.

Organizational Learning Versus Training

It is easy to assume that learning in organizations is simply about training and education programs. Nonprofits have been fairly good about providing training and educational opportunities for their employees. They do this through their own human resources departments, local university programs, management support organizations, professional associations, and consultants. An employee attends a half-day workshop on grant writing given by a local university. An employee returns to school to finish a Master's in Social Work degree. A board member attends a one-day program on the fiduciary responsibility of board members offered by the state's association for nonprofits. Each of these examples is a potentially beneficial individual learning opportunity.

However, individual training and education, although helpful, are not necessarily the kind of learning that results in enhanced organizational effectiveness. Nonprofits need to be continually learning as a total organization; learning how to improve performance and learning how to learn how to improve performance.

Levels of Learning

In high-performing nonprofits, four levels of learning occur simultaneously: individual learning, team learning, whole organization learning, and community learning. The first three levels are internally focused. The fourth level, community, is externally focused and is one of the primary ways in which nonprofits are different from other types of organizations. They have an obligation to improve the quality of life in a community wider than just their own organizations. The next four chapters explain these four levels in more depth; an overview is provided here.

Individual Learning

Individual learning occurs as each person acquires the knowledge, develops the skills, and adopts the attitudes and beliefs that will help the organization succeed (however success is defined). Individual learning prepares employees and volunteers for the inevitable changes that will occur in the goals and work processes of the organization. In addition, individual learning creates greater self-awareness in order for each person to become a more effective human being. This is Senge's (1990) notion of personal mastery. Goleman (1998) calls this developing emotional intelligence. It is the self-awareness and sense of competence that allows one to take risks, accept feedback, learn from successes and mistakes, relate effectively to others, and stay focused on personal goals.

Of course, all learning occurs first within individuals. But to the extent that the collective know-how and know-why (Kim, 1993a) of individuals changes the culture, behavior, and effectiveness of the group or whole organization, the group or organization can be said to be learning. For example, you and each person on your team might have learned how to prepare and monitor a budget, but figuring out how best to handle a major reduction in revenue (e.g., discontinuation of a foundation grant) requires the synergistic thinking of the entire team. It is not the sum of the individual learning, but the creativity and knowledge that comes from the team members learning together that results in a successful solution.

Team Learning

Team learning occurs as the members of a group discover together how best to contribute to the performance of the group as a whole.

They learn from and about each other, how to work effectively as a group, and how to apply that knowledge to achieving the purposes of the group. Not all groups in the workplace are teams (Katzenbach & Smith, 1993), but all groups can achieve some group learning. Because of their shared goals and the value they put on member interaction, teams achieve more group learning than other types of work groups.

Team learning occurs as "a continuous process by which team members acquire knowledge about the larger organization, the team, and the individual team members" (Russ-Eft, Preskill, & Sleezer, 1997, p. 139). This knowledge resides with the team as a whole and not with any single individual. It is what maximizes the effectiveness of the team as everyone on the team works toward shared goals and shared processes for achieving those goals.

Whole Organization Learning

Whole organization learning is the "ongoing processes and integrated systems that facilitate individuals' and teams' ability to learn, grow, and change as a result of organizational experiences" (Russ-Eft et al., 1997, p. 268). This occurs when managers can eliminate boundaries that prevent the free flow of information across the organization. You should ask yourself, "What can I do to help this organization learn about itself; learn what results in new knowledge, skills, attitudes, and beliefs; and learn how to create a culture of learning? How can I be a 'merchant of light' (Rubin, 1998), illuminating a challenge so that others can see?"

Whole organization learning is achieving a shared understanding throughout the organization and creating the capacity throughout the organization to improve processes and achieve strategic goals. Marquardt (1996) had the whole organization in mind when he said that

> organizational learning occurs through the shared insights, knowledge, and mental models of members of the organization. . . . Organizational learning builds on past knowledge and experience—that is, on organizational memory which depends on institutional mechanisms (e.g., policies, strategies, and explicit models) used to retain knowledge. (p. 22)

Whole organization learning is about building the capacity of large, complex organizations to change continuously. The American Red Cross changed its mission to encompass not just blood banks and disaster relief but also emergency prevention and training. Boys and Girls Clubs changed from offering only after-school recreation programs to also offering career development for disadvantaged youth. A large, private foundation changed from a preoccupation with "getting the money out the door" to a commitment to be a facilitator of change for the betterment of communities. A large university hospital changed from doctors and research first to patients and families first. Each of these organizations has had to learn how to become a different organization in order to achieve its new goals.

Community Learning

Nonprofits have a special role to play in helping communities learn how to build their capacity to improve the quality of life for all citizens. Nonprofits already have a vested interest in quality-of-life issues, and often they are perceived as neutral actors in local issues. This puts them in a position to bring key stakeholders to the table to work on these issues.

The community of a nonprofit is defined broadly as the set of external constituencies. The community for a food bank is defined by geography. The community for a symphony is defined by patrons. The community for a professional association is its members.

With the help of nonprofits, communities can develop processes to evaluate their current state, plan for change, and build consensus around contentious issues. For example, geographic areas—such as towns, cities, municipalities, metropolitan regions, and even states—can learn how to improve social services, provide education for all youth, protect the environment, ensure health care for everyone, and create livable spaces. They can assess the gap between where they are and where they want to be, set goals for what they want to achieve as a community, and build the capacity to continue to confront new challenges that they will face.

Learning How to Learn

Think of a skill that you have tried to learn recently. A musical instrument? A new computer program? A dance step? Cross-country skiing or inline skating? How did you approach the task of learning? Did you read about it first or discuss it with experts? Did you watch or listen to others doing it? Did you carefully analyze their behavior, or did you fix a mental image of the skill in your mind? Did you hire a coach or attend a class? Or, did you just start doing it, learning from trial and error?

Each of these methods represents different ways in which individuals prefer to learn a new skill. There is no one right way, just different ways that individuals prefer depending on life experiences, the way individuals process information in their brains, the specific circumstances of the learning, and attitudes toward the skill. You can maximize organizational learning by being aware of how employees and volunteers prefer to learn in a given situation and helping them to use a variety of methods to facilitate their learning. This is helping them learn how to learn.

Start by noticing how you learn best in different situations, what the conditions are, and why you learn best under those conditions. This means taking a mental step back from the learning process and analyzing what it is about the process that helps you learn and what the barriers are to your learning. As an individual, maybe the best way for you to learn how to use new accounting software is by trial and error. You like to start using the package in your work and figuring it out as you go along. Maybe the best way for you to learn how to give performance feedback to someone you supervise is to role-play the situation with an experienced coach who will then observe your interaction with the employee and evaluate your actions.

When you understand your own learning style, you can help others learn how to learn about

- themselves
- interacting effectively with others
- technical skills to do their jobs
- the organization's vision, mission, values, guiding principles, and strategic goals
- their customers, clients, volunteers, and other stakeholders
- business processes
- the external environment
- the future and how it will affect their activities.

You can help by showing others how their individual behaviors can contribute unintentionally to the organization's problems (Argyris, 1991). For example, senior managers who deny their own responsibility for problems in the face of subordinates' honest feedback to the contrary send a message that the organization does not value individual learning and improvement. Help these managers become aware of the negative influence they can have on the organization.

Small groups, whether work groups or teams, need to learn how to learn about working effectively as a group. You have probably participated in many groups that were given an assignment and proceeded through that task without attending to the processes and internal dynamics of the group that make learning possible. These groups are destined to repeat their failures and not improve on their weaknesses. They are not able to take full advantage of their strengths. This goes for the process of interacting and making decisions as well as performing the actual task. Some boards of directors will meet monthly for years, going through the same agenda each time, never discussing underlying assumptions, strategic direction, or leadership issues, even while the nonprofit is going into deep debt, losing experienced employees, and creating a negative image in the community. These boards have not learned how to learn together, and therefore, they cannot change. For example, they could learn by each person making known to the group his or her understanding of the group's purpose and by developing a shared meaning of their work together.

The organization, as a whole, needs to learn how to learn. You have heard the complaints:

"We keep reinventing the wheel."

"The left hand doesn't know what the right hand is doing."

"They are just rearranging the deck chairs on the *Titanic*."

Sound familiar? These are metaphors for an organization that hasn't learned how to reach its potential. To learn, an organization must value and support generative learning. It can do this by creating mechanisms and procedures for individuals and groups to share their knowledge with each other, documenting and recording the experiences of people across the organization so that everyone's knowledge and skills are accessible to the entire organization, and reflecting honestly across the whole organization on what people have done and how effectively they have done it. Your job is to help your organization appreciate the need for individual, small group, whole organization, and community learning and to contribute to creating a learning culture.

Bruno Laporte and Ron Kim talk about the challenges of creating a learning culture at the World Bank (Bellanet, 2002). In response to the question "What are the biggest obstacles you have encountered?" they said,

> Culture. Trying to get people to recognize the value of sharing knowledge and learning from each other within the organization. Asking questions when they don't know something, and sharing what they do know. Looking at the accumulated knowledge, and recognizing the value of the free-flow of knowledge within the organization. We are trying to address that in a number of ways: changing formal evaluation systems; recognition and awards; knowledge fairs; stories to highlight behaviour of teams; and on the communication side—why/how KM [knowledge management] is beneficial.
>
> This is an ongoing task. It takes more than 5 years to change the behaviour of an entire organization. However, we have seen significant changes moving from an inward-looking institution to make it more open to looking outside the organization and sharing more of what the Bank knows with external partners.

This World Bank experience demonstrates that creating a culture of learning is the kind of change that does not happen overnight. People need to think and behave quite differently from how they have in the past. Let's look at some of the ways you can shape a learning culture through communication, leadership, performance incentives, and physical environment.

Communication

Often what we think to be good interpersonal communication is actually a barrier to learning. Managers tend to say and do things to keep morale high, to be considerate and positive, and to not open Pandora's box of problems. But, in effect, they are preventing employees from confronting problems and learning from mistakes. Managers' behavior often discourages asking questions about the underlying values and rationale for organizational decisions and practices. For the sake of harmony, bad practice goes unexamined. It is understandable. People do not want to experience embarrassment, loss of control, tension, and unhappiness in the workplace. However, the cost of avoiding problems is enormous. The organization cannot learn from its own behavior (Argyris, 1994).

To avoid these defensive routines, ask the hard questions and encourage others to do the same. Confront the hard facts and sensitive feelings. Ask, "What goes on in this organization that prevents us from questioning these practices and getting them corrected or eliminated?" and "What can we do to bring about a change?"

Afterwards, do not punish people for being open and honest when you hear their responses. You may be unaware that you are doing this, so be on your guard. If an employee takes a risk and tries something new and fails, focus on what was learned, not on what went wrong. If an employee challenges a practice that you started or you have supported, do not immediately try to think of reasons why the employee's thinking is wrong. Try to find ways in which you can incorporate the employee's ideas. If an employee asks, "Why do we continue to offer a service that is losing money?" do not say it is because that is what management wants. Find out the rationale and report this back to the employee who asked the question. Focusing on what went wrong, trying to find error in someone's ideas, and shifting blame are all examples of reactions that feel like punishment to the person at the receiving end.

Keep in mind the principles of dialogue presented elsewhere in this book. Try to understand the other person's point of view rather than convince that person of your position. Listen to each other, surface underlying assumptions and beliefs, and weave connections among ideas. Look for clarity. Do not look for solutions. Agreement is not important; what is important is listening to all ideas and opinions.

Once you fully understand the person's ideas and suggestions, demonstrate that you value this openness and honesty by acting on what was said. Communicate back to the person that the ideas and suggestions had an influence. Maybe they affected your thinking or were part of a discussion among managers, or maybe they actually changed the practice. Implementing the suggestion is not as important as letting the employee know that you listened, you valued their comments, and that the lines of communication are still open between you.

Leadership

When people say "leadership," what do they mean?

Most employees are not looking for another Gandhi or Churchill. For the most part, they just want someone who will help them be successful without a lot of pain. Unfortunately, what they usually get is someone who gets a lot of *things* done but does not help individuals, teams, the whole organization, and community with their learning.

A hierarchical, command-and-control leadership style is still the predominant style in all types of organizations today, regardless of values and mission. Although effective in certain situations, such as when efficiency and accountability are paramount, this style is generally a barrier to organizational learning. This style closes off vital input from the various parts of the organization and from outside. Hierarchical leaders put energy into maintaining the lines of authority and communication represented by the organizational chart and not into seeking and using information from inside and outside of one's functional area (Rummler & Brache, 1990).

When stability was valued more than change, loyalty more than quality, similarities more than differences, and individuality more than teamwork, then the command-and-control style of leadership was effective. That style has dominated management behavior since the Industrial Revolution. Today, regardless of rhetoric to the contrary, that style still dominates management. However, in the current environment, and particularly in order to achieve organizational learning, a different kind of nonprofit leader is needed.

As Drucker (1996) has said,

All effective leaders . . . know four simple things: 1. The only definition of a leader is someone who has followers. Some people are thinkers. Some are prophets. Both roles are important and badly needed. But without followers, there can be no leaders. 2. An effective leader is not someone who is loved or admired. He or she is someone whose followers do the right things. Popularity is not leadership. Results are. 3. Leaders are highly visible. They therefore set examples. 4. Leadership is not rank, privileges, titles, or money. It is responsibility. (p. xii)

Drucker is saying that the command-and-control style of leadership has given way to a leader who is respected, inspires right action, is visible, and takes responsibility.

Leadership of organizational learning can come from anyone at any level in a nonprofit. The model for this kind of behavior should come from the top of the organization, but others must step forward from time to time and provide this leadership when and where it is needed. An office assistant who says, "Let's try the new client database for 30 days, monitor its usefulness, and then come together and decide if we want to continue with it" is leading organizational learning. A manager who forms a team of people from across the organization to evaluate a pilot test of a new program and make improvements before widespread implementation is leading organizational learning. A trustee who engages the board in a discussion of indicators the organization should use to determine overall effectiveness is leading organizational learning.

For leadership to make a difference in organizational learning, it must be linked to the outcomes that the particular organization needs for success. These outcomes are specific performance improvements of the individual, team, organization, or community. This conceptual link between leadership and results for the organization should be made apparent to all stakeholders. Ask yourself these questions:

- What are the long-term outcomes that will indicate that the organization is successful? (Examples of indicators of success: revenue, sustainability, and accomplishment of mission.)
- What are the short-term objectives that, if achieved, will lead to these long-term outcomes? (Examples of indicators of progress: number of participants in programs, customer satisfaction, reputation in community, and efficiency of services.)
- What work processes need to be improved to achieve these organizational objectives?
- What are the critical job tasks that leaders in this organization must do to improve these work processes?
- What knowledge, skills, and attitudes do leaders in this organization need in order to perform these critical job tasks?

When the answers to these questions are aligned, you have a map that explains performance in your organization. You have a way to monitor learning and performance improvement. See the logic model description in Chapter 9.

Performance Incentives

According to Tobin (1998), effective organizations encourage learning

> by enabling and facilitating the exchange of knowledge and ideas and by empowering employees to try new ideas. . . . If a new idea doesn't work out, the employee is rewarded for a thoughtful, well-conceived attempt at improvement—not punished for failing. Managers in these organizations coach employees and reinforce their learning to ensure that new ideas are properly applied to the job to add value to the employee's work. (p. 2)

Too often, the creativity and risk taking involved in trying new ideas are punished, not rewarded. It is not intentional, but leaders sometimes apply controls to situations that, in effect, send a contradictory message. For example, a foundation that said it wanted to encourage risk taking and be the "R&D for nonprofits" had appropriation requests denied by its board of trustees, from a few thousand dollars to multimillion-dollar projects. The lore of the organization held that anything too innovative or sensitive, that might create a negative response in the wider community, would be rejected by the trustees. True or not, this belief contributed to a culture that was incompatible with learning from truly creative and adventurous endeavors.

The right incentives must be in place to encourage learning. Incentives take many forms: money; promotions; new titles; new responsibilities; training and development; new work opportunities; public recognition; and probably the most overlooked incentive, just saying, "Good job." The right incentive depends on the people being rewarded. Different people respond differently to different incentives in different situations. Whatever the incentive, for maximum effect, the key is to tie it clearly to learning through words and behavior. Staff and volunteers need to see the connection between their learning and the rewards. For example, if you want employees to learn how to work in a team, you must give team members the authority to make decisions and show your support for them by accepting the consequences of those decisions. Let the group try and fail or try and succeed. Either way, they have the opportunity for learning. Give recognition to the learning, not just the successes.

Physical Environment

Is the physical environment of the workplace conducive to learning? Does the arrangement of workspaces and the foot traffic flow facilitate communication among employees? Are the people who need to learn from each other coming into frequent contact?

Most workplace learning occurs from informal interactions that occur because of proximity. Casual hallway conversations among coworkers might lead to comparing their experiences with a new process. Chance meetings between managers might result in discussing a new strategy for dealing with a supervision problem. Free-flowing, lunchtime discussions among work team members might generate an innovation in how they do their work together.

Tom Peters (1992) wrote in *Liberation Management*:

> Physical location issues are neither plain nor vanilla. In fact, space management may well be the most ignored—and most powerful—tool for inducing cultural change, speeding up innovation projects and enhancing the learning process in far-flung organizations. While we fret ceaselessly about facilities issues such as office square footage allotted to various ranks, we all but ignore the key strategic issue—the parameters of intermingling. (p. 413)

Much traditional work space is designed for maximum control and maintenance of hierarchy. Line and lower-level workers are on the inside, maybe in cubicles or in an open space, whereas senior managers and executives are in outer offices with one window on employees and one window on the outside world. The higher your rank in the organization, the larger your office and the more sunlight. But if we asked "What is the best design for organizational learning?" we would end up with a much different configuration and allocation of space. We would design for maximum interaction of team members and among staff and volunteers who need to share information, make decisions, and solve problems together.

Small, entrepreneurial nonprofits that are short on space but long on commitment will have staff who are constantly sharing information with each other. This is simply because of their close proximity and desire to make a difference. As these organizations grow and require more space and operational controls, they are challenged to arrange the workspace so that sharing of information and learning from each other continues. One nonprofit, which started as a few idealistic individuals working in close proximity and, because of growth, had to move to larger office space five times over a 10-year period, discovered that each of these locations had a different impact on the quality of collective learning. The difference ranged from minimal interaction to intense interaction and learning, depending on the configuration of work spaces.

On an individual level, the workplace should accommodate the wide range of differences in how people learn. At times, some people need quiet and solitude. At other times, some people need contact with others and benefit from being surrounded by activity. Some people can handle and even thrive when there is distraction, and others cannot get anything done when they are constantly interrupted.

On a small group level, the workplace should accommodate the need for face-to-face interaction, the need for cross-functional interaction, the need for varying kinds of spaces in which to meet, and the need for space availability on short notice.

On a whole organization level, the workplace structure should be a visible statement that reinforces the values espoused by the organization. If organizational learning is valued, access to information, people, and technology that everyone needs in order to contribute to achieving the business goals should be evident in the design and management of the facility. Space and its use make a very powerful statement about who and what is valued by the organization.

You might not have authority to build a new facility, but you can try to influence how interior spaces are designed and used. As with any task outside of your experience, you should seek help from an expert (e.g., interior designer). Using the benchmarking method, you can see many good ideas implemented at other companies. The major office systems companies (such as Steelcase, Haworth, and Herman Miller) will be especially open to showing you examples of how work space can be designed to facilitate interaction and teamwork among employees.

Use a decision-making process to design your workplace. Relate the design to the values and goals of your organization (O'Mara, 1999). You can use the design problem to turn employees' attention to the future and the organization's strategic direction. You can ask, "If we have to live in this space for the next 5 years, what design would maximize our learning and performance?"

The design and management of the workplace contributes to organizational learning if you

- make space considerations part of strategic planning
- use an open office plan with work areas dedicated to teams whenever appropriate
- provide space for team members to meet formally whenever a meeting is necessary
- arrange people and offices so that informal, chance contacts are frequent
- locate the technology so that employees have access when and where they need it
- give employees control over the comfort of their office environment (such as lighting, temperature, and furniture) whenever possible
- minimize noise and visual distractions for those employees for whom these interfere with their effectiveness.

These strategies have proved effective in a wide variety of organizations (American Society of Interior Designers, 1998). However, no one can tell you what will work best in your organization. You have to be willing to experiment: Try a strategy, evaluate its impact on learning, make changes if it does not have the impact you want, and try again. Take the time. There are no quick fixes.

Actions for Developing a Learning Culture

Whether you are focusing on communication, leadership, performance incentives, or physical environment to create a culture of learning, the key is ongoing self-evaluation. That is, continuously putting your nonprofit in front of a mirror and asking, "Are we where we want to be as an organization, and if not, what do we have to do to get there?" External evaluation consultants can assist you with answering this from time to time, but this process of feedback and reflection does not necessarily depend on external help. Much can be done with the staff and resources within your organization.

Here are some activities that can create and maintain a culture that is conducive to learning:

1. Make highly visible, dramatic changes that are symbolic, as well as substantive, of a learning culture in the organization.

2. Ensure that values demonstrated in everyday actions are consistent with espoused values of learning. Talk about this alignment of values with your employees.

3. Assess and compare the perceived current culture with the desired learning culture.

4. Develop a shared plan with board members and staff for what the organization must do to move from the current culture to the desired learning culture.

5. Allow employees to dedicate time to formal and informal learning that will enhance their capacity to do their work effectively.

6. Develop learning events that are explicitly linked to the strategic goals of the organization.

7. Create ceremonies that give recognition to individual and team learning.

8. Make the artifacts of learning visible to employees, such as a library, spaces for formal and informal conversations among employees, benefits that support education, and computer access to just-in-time information.

9. Praise individuals and groups that use learning as one of their indicators of success.

Here are two tools you can use to promote organizational learning. First, effective learning in your organization begins with internalizing a set of principles related to systemic change. Check your nonprofit's readiness for system-wide, organizational learning by using the Organizational Learning Readiness Worksheet (see Tool 3.1). Bring together employees and volunteers (either everyone in a small non-profit or a cross-functional group within a large nonprofit). Ask individuals to fill out the form for themselves. Then ask the group, "Do we aspire to this principle?" "What do we do as an organization

Tool 3.1	Organizational Learning Readiness Worksheet			
To what extent is each of these principles characteristic of your organization? Check the number that best represents what you observe in your organization. 　　1 = Not at all; never see it 　　2 = Partly characteristic; occasionally see evidence 　　3 = Strongly characteristic; evidence all around us				
Principle		*1*	*2*	*3*
1. We integrate and align our organization's mission, people, processes, resources, structures, and culture.				
2. Each of our organization's activities is an element of a process that is continuously improved through knowledge enhancement.				
3. We don't rely on quick fixes to our performance deficits.				
4. Learning is continuous over the long term in order to achieve meaningful results.				
5. Learning is leveraged so that relatively small interventions result in long-term major changes for the organization.				
6. Each of our employees and volunteers is responsible for the system in which he or she works.				
7. The collective learning of all employees and volunteers is an essential aspect of capacity building.				

that is consistent with this principle?" "What can we do to make this principle part of our culture?" Discuss their answers. Return to these questions periodically with the same group to assess progress.

The implication of holding these beliefs is that learning alliances must be formed with supervisors; among the various departments, programs, and units in your organization; and with your clients and partner organizations. Over time, effective learning alliances will result in accumulated knowledge. The accumulated knowledge of an organization is one of its most valuable assets. This knowledge is as important to a nonprofit as its property; donations; funding sources; products and services; and the loyalty of employees, volunteers, and clients.

Another tool you can use to assess the status of your learning culture is the Organizational Learning Self-Audit (Tool 3.2). How do you know if your nonprofit is doing what it can to learn and improve? This tool can be used to do a quick status check.

Ask a cross-section of employees and volunteers in your organization to fill out this self-audit with you. Answer these questions for your organization as a whole. Post the group's responses on a chart for everyone in the group to see, and then discuss your responses and their implications. Look for similarities and differences in the way people responded. What made group members respond the way they did to each statement? Report a summary of the group's responses to the entire organization, and invite comments from staff and volunteers. Use this information in planning initiatives to improve organizational learning.

Summary

This chapter has defined what is meant by "a culture of learning" and explained how this culture contributes to building an effective organization. A culture of learning is an environment that supports and encourages the collective discovery, sharing, and application of knowledge. Learning is manifested in every aspect of organizational life. Staff and volunteers are continuously learning as individuals, in teams (and other small work groups), as a whole organization, and in relation to their communities. A learning culture can be developed through communication and leadership. The next chapter goes into depth about the first level of a learning culture: individual learning.

Tool 3.2 Organizational Learning Self-Audit

Indicate to what extent you agree with each of the statements listed below. Check the response option on the right that is closest to what you believe about your organization.

Organizational Learning Statement	Strongly Agree	Agree	Neither Agree Nor Disagree	Disagree	Strongly Disagree
1. This organization is constantly learning how to improve its own performance.					
2. Gathering feedback and reflecting on that information is commonly done in this organization.					
3. Managers who support individual and team learning are rewarded for doing so.					
4. We are constantly trying to learn how to have more effective meetings, events, and projects.					
5. Experimentation and risk taking for the purpose of learning are supported and not punished.					
6. Physical spaces of offices and service areas are designed for optimum learning among individuals and teams.					
7. Individuals understand what they need to learn in order to help the organization be successful.					
8. Individuals are encouraged to enhance their ability to help the organization be successful.					
9. Managers, coaches, and mentors help individuals develop and implement learning plans.					

Organizational Learning Statement	Strongly Agree	Agree	Neither Agree Nor Disagree	Disagree	Strongly Disagree
10. Training programs are designed to help individuals achieve their learning goals.					
11. Individuals receive frequent formal and informal feedback on their job performance.					
12. Individuals discuss with their supervisors what they need to learn to improve their performance.					
13. Team members help each other learn from their successes and failures.					
14. Information is constantly shared among team members.					
15. Training programs are designed to help teams achieve their learning goals.					
16. Teams are constantly developing new, more effective ways of working as a group.					
17. The organization gathers feedback from its customers and stakeholders for the purpose of learning.					
18. Each department/unit informs other departments about what is being learned.					
19. The organization as a whole works at developing more effective ways to solve problems and make decisions.					
20. The organization is open to learning from the wider community that it serves.					

4

Individual Learning

We now accept the fact that learning is a lifelong process of keeping abreast of change. And the most pressing task is to teach people how to learn.

—Peter Drucker

A learning culture is an environment in which individual learning, team learning, whole organization learning, and community learning are nurtured. This chapter is an exploration of the first level of learning in that culture—individual learning. Learning at this level is the foundation for collective learning that occurs in high-performing teams and high-performing organizations.

Definition of Learning at the Individual Level

Learning at the individual level in an organization occurs when a person acquires new knowledge, skills, attitudes, and beliefs that change the way that person perceives the world, understands information, and performs on the job, and this learning contributes to organizational performance. This learning is the development of three kinds of abilities: (a) technical abilities, such as using an Excel spreadsheet or arranging shelter for a homeless person; (b) relationship abilities, such as employee coaching or leading a team meeting; and

(c) learning-how-to-learn abilities, such as applying the action learning method. Not only is an individual learner able to perform the technical skills of a job, but that person relates effectively to others and knows how to keep on learning.

Learning at the individual level is a shared responsibility between individuals and the organization as a whole. It is the obligation of employees and volunteers to take charge of their own development, and it is the obligation of the organization to offer an environment conducive to learning.

We learn by paying attention to our environment and the people and information around us, and then by applying what we know. By touching a hot stove, we learn to stay away from burners when they have recently been used. If we read in a magazine about a new fitness exercise to strengthen back muscles, we can learn by practicing that technique at home. If a friend gives us advice on how to handle a difficult conversation with a family member, we can learn by trying out this advice, thus developing a more effective way of inter-acting with other people. These are examples of common, day-to-day occurrences of individual learning. Learning also occurs through more formal training programs in which there is exposure to new information and practicing of new skills.

Organizational learning at the individual level has a focus on strengthening the organization. This kind of learning is about

- discovering how you work and learn best
- achieving greater awareness of your own values and goals
- achieving greater awareness of what you do well and what you need to improve
- balancing work, family, and leisure activities
- knowing how you fit into the direction of the organization
- knowing what you have to do to help the organization succeed
- creating new approaches to old problems

As you can see from this list, you are building your capacity to contribute to achieving the goals of the organization. This kind of learning helps an employee become a more effective member of the organization. But it is also learning with the intent of building the overall capacity of the organization to reach its potential.

Therefore, this kind of learning requires alignment. That is, what is being learned must be consistent with intended results for the organization. For example, you might learn project management skills because you have the responsibility to put on a large fundraising event that is critical to supporting programs for the next year. You should not be learning project management skills simply because Project Management 101 has openings, or you have money in your budget, or everyone else is doing it. This learning is not just for the sake of self-improvement, simply out of personal interest, or because the topic is the latest fad. Organizational learning at the individual level should contribute directly to making the organization successful.

Feedback and Reflection

Individual learning in organizations is a social process. It is difficult to do without feedback from others and reflection with others. Gathering feedback begins with these basic questions.

- What happened?
- What were you trying to do?
- What results did you want?
- What were the actual results?
- What could have been done better?
- How would you improve things next time?

Ask yourself, or even better, ask someone else to ask you these questions. Think about the meaning of your answers. Reflection is the process of finding useful meaning in the answers. Asking the questions and then reflecting on the answers, putting this information in front of you to see yourself in the data, and thinking about what that means to you and your own behavior turn information into knowledge and knowledge into wisdom.

Reflection by yourself is a start but can give you a distorted understanding of the situation. It is much like looking in a mirror and not seeing yourself as others see you. How we see our reflection is influenced by our expectations and judgment of ourselves. Engaging others in your reflection activity is likely to produce more accurate and useful learning.

Hallie Preskill and Rosalie T. Torres (1999) call the process of reflection with the help of others *evaluative inquiry*:

> Evaluative inquiry represents an emphasis on understanding each other in order to understand larger organizational challenges. Consequently, inquiry becomes a social and communal activity in which critical organizational issues are constructed by a varied and broadly based community of inquirers. These issues are subjected to continuous reconsideration and reexamination through a dialogic process involving many diverse participants. In essence, evaluative inquiry is about practical wisdom and organization members deliberating about what is good and expedient, with an emphasis on using data to inform learning and action. (p. 2)

In order for this kind of "social and communal" questioning to occur, the organization must create an environment that is safe for inquiry. Staff and volunteers will not engage in this self-critical behavior unless they believe that it is encouraged and valued, as opposed to discouraged and avoided.

Negative cultural cues regarding reflective inquiry can be subtle or overt. Reflective inquiry is discouraged by managers when they do not allow time for reflection and never ask, "How are we doing?" "What are we learning?" "What should we do differently?" They never challenge underlying assumptions. They move frantically from one problem to the next without ever asking, "What do we have to change to prevent these problems from happening over and over again?" and "Is this what we should be doing in the first place?" Reflective inquiry is also discouraged by managers when they are not receptive to new ideas or different ways of thinking about a problem. They might say, "We have been developing our budgets this way for 20 years; no need to change now."

As a manager of a nonprofit, you play an important role in facilitating reflective inquiry in others. If your organization has a training department, it can be a useful resource in helping you ask learning questions. However, as a manager, you are a critical instrument in the learning process for the employees you supervise. Your support for an employee's learning before, during, and after exposure to new information is critical to organizational learning. Learning will be optimized if you form an alliance with individuals around their learning and make it an essential part of their work (Brinkerhoff & Gill, 1994). In this role, you are their learning partner and coach.

Following are steps you can take to form and maintain this alliance:

1. Discuss what the employee (or volunteer) needs to learn in order to help your department or program achieve its objectives and the organization's strategic goals.

2. Agree on a set of learning objectives for the staff member. You might ask the person to prepare a list of learning objectives and then bring that list to you for discussion.

3. Decide together what will indicate that the learning has been achieved.

4. Review the methods for learning and decide together which methods might be most effective in helping this person learn.

5. Write an individualized learning plan with this person.

6. Help the staff member arrange to use appropriate resources in a just-in-time manner.

7. Plan frequent, regular, and brief meetings to discuss progress toward goals and any needed modifications in the process.

8. Change the learning process as goals and conditions change.

In essence, guide and support this person through the learning process. Hold up the reflective-inquiry mirror and encourage the employee (or volunteer) to look at his or her behavior in relation to organizational events. Help the person ask the tough questions. By taking these steps, you will focus the person's learning on what is most important for the organization, and learning will occur more quickly and be more sustainable than if the learner had to do this in isolation. As a social process, individual learning in organizations needs the give-and-take that you can provide.

Methods

The method used for learning at the individual level should fit the learning objective. Decide what is to be learned first, and then design the way it will be learned.

Some of the more commonly used methods are described below. Each of these methods uses reflective inquiry: asking questions, collecting data (answers to the questions), making sense of the data, and using this information to make decisions.

To have maximum effect, these methods must be tailored to the needs of each learner. Learners should work with their supervisors to agree to goals and performance outcomes for the activity. Ask learners: "What information do you want to take from this experience?" "How will you apply this knowledge on the job?" "How will we know that it has had a positive effect?" Having this kind of plan is critical to ensuring that learning has a useful impact. Having many people in an organization learn how to use these methods builds the capacity of that organization.

Instructor-Led Classroom Seminars, Workshops, and Courses

You can find this traditional format offered locally through educational institutions, at the state level by state associations, at the national level by national associations, by independent trainers, and maybe in your organization by internal trainers. These programs might have topics such as fundraising, grant writing, public relations and communication, leadership, board development, program evaluation, strategic planning, project management, diversity, or any of a myriad of other topics.

If an instructor-led classroom learning experience is the appropriate method, then much upfront planning is essential. Classroom instruction, as with all other learning methods, requires careful design. An entire discipline of study has grown up in the past 25 years around instructional system design (Richey, 1986). Involve instructional-design professionals along with the content experts when using this method. You will want them to collaborate to ensure that learning needs are identified; that the context for learning is taken into consideration; that appropriate learning objectives are set; that a course curriculum is developed to address the breadth of learning that is needed; that the classroom experience conveys the knowledge, skills, attitudes, and beliefs necessary for success; that the learners are given adequate feedback to help them improve; and that there is adequate follow-up to ensure effective application on the job.

To maximize learning, the instruction must be designed to achieve specific learning objectives aligned with organizational goals. These objectives give the instruction direction, motivate learners, shape the content and methods of instruction, and are the criteria for assessing effectiveness of the instruction. Therefore, the first step in instructional design is to determine learning objectives. Involve yourself in answering these key questions:

- What competencies do employees and volunteers need to have in order to help this organization achieve its strategic goals?
- What specifically (knowledge, skills, attitudes, and beliefs) do employees and volunteers need to be able to do?
- What is the best way to achieve these objectives?
- How will I know that this learning has occurred?

Whether for specific job skills or for learning to work more effectively with others and for the organization as a whole, the process of creating an effective instructional program has four phases:

Phase 1: Formulate learning goals. Decide what knowledge, skills, attitudes, and beliefs (KSABs) are needed by staff to help the organization become successful. Identify indicators that you will measure to know if these KSABs have been applied successfully.

Phase 2: Plan learning strategies. Decide which learning methods will result in the outcomes necessary for achieving the organization's goals.

Phase 3: Implement learning methods. Prepare the learner for learning. Keep the focus on the learning outcomes. Adjust methods to ensure that you achieve the desired outcomes.

Phase 4: Support performance improvement. Reinforce application of learning to the workplace. Provide refresher learning events, job aids, and feedback as needed. Remove organizational barriers (e.g., lack of on-the-job opportunities) to applying new skills. (Brinkerhoff & Gill, 1994)

Keep in mind that this method is not always the answer to individual learning and performance improvement. With a misguided sense of what is good educational practice, probably a result of our own school experiences, organizations rely too much on instructor-led, classroom-based training. Surveys consistently estimate that 80% to 90% of all training in organizations is delivered in this way. As the saying goes, "To a hammer, everything looks like a nail." If you equate learning with classroom instruction, then every learning need is met with a course, seminar, or workshop.

Even our language prevents us from thinking of other methods of helping people learn. "Training" has become a synonym for instructor-led, classroom-based experiences, when in fact, other methods might be much more effective, depending on what needs to be learned and the learning style of an employee or volunteer.

Instructor-led classroom experiences are indicated for individual learning only when the instructor has expert knowledge that the learners need to know and this knowledge cannot be disseminated in any other way; when the individual learners will benefit from learning in a directed group environment; and when the learners will have an immediate opportunity to apply the new knowledge, skills, attitudes, or beliefs to their work. Often, the application of this method of learning does not meet these criteria. For example, some content, such as team building, is best taught experientially with an intact team on the job, and some employees and volunteers learn best when they are engaged interactively with the teacher rather than listening passively in a classroom.

The decision to use the instructor-led, classroom-based teaching format is often made on the basis of tradition (we have always done it this way), efficiency (we can get everyone through in a short time), expediency (we already have the materials and instructors for the program), convenience (the local United Way agency is offering the course), or cost (the local community college offers the course for only $50). These might be good administrative reasons to use the classroom approach, but they are not good learning reasons. Most of what is taught in this way is not retained by learners.

Sometimes, however, given the content and given the learning styles of staff and volunteers, this format is optimal. Select this method cautiously, use the method sparingly, and design it well. Design for learning and sustained performance improvement. Keep in mind these principles of adult learning:

1. No two people learn in exactly the same way. Instruction should be adapted to the way adults learn.

2. Employees can be ordered to do something new, but they cannot be forced to learn. Adults will resist being required to learn something, especially if they don't agree with the reason for it.

3. Adults are motivated to learn by significant work and life changes and believing that what they will learn will help them cope with those changes. Adults are driven by meaningful work that makes a difference in the lives of others.

4. For some adults, learning is its own reward, but for most, learning is a means to an end. Some adults won't learn unless they can see how it will lead to meaningful results.

5. Enhanced self-esteem and pleasure are strong secondary motivators of learning. Adults want to feel better about themselves and enjoy what they are doing.

6. Adults have teachable moments, when the timing of learning is critical to its success and retention. Adults often know their optimal times for learning.

7. Staff want the opportunity to apply newly learned knowledge and skills to relevant problems in the organization. Adults want to use what they have learned to make a difference.

8. Adults learn best when they can integrate new information with what they already know. Employees and volunteers have considerable experience that provides an important context for their own learning.

9. Fast-paced, complex, and unusual learning tasks interfere with learning for adults. This might be generation-specific, but many adults have trouble adjusting to the MTV style and Internet speed of newer technologies.

10. Adults tend to let their own errors affect their self-esteem, and that causes them to avoid risk by resorting to old ways of doing things. They will stay with what they know rather than expose themselves to possible failure and embarrassment.

11. Adults prefer to have a say about the design and direction of their learning experiences. They want to feel a sense of control over the situation.

12. Adults prefer learning experiences that provide opportunities for interaction with their peers. They want to know how they compare to, what they can learn from, and how to stay connected to others.

People do not maximize their learning from formal training events unless they are prepared and motivated to learn before the event, their learning is reinforced and applied, and they are given feedback on their progress during and after the event. Although a simplification of the process, think of learning as having a before, during, and after phase in relation to the content to be learned. For example, let's say that your organization needs to do a better job of managing its finances. Simply sending employees to a financial management workshop where they are taught about balance sheets, cash flow analysis, financial planning, and the use of software to manage budgets is nice, but not sufficient. Employees must be prepared for learning about financial management before the training event, in the sense of setting learning goals for themselves and knowing how this competency will help the organization achieve its goals, they must be assisted in applying financial management to the organization shortly after the training event, and they must be given feedback on performance. Otherwise, employees will not learn what they need to learn and will not retain that learning. The result will be a waste of time and money.

Personal Visioning

We are driven by goals. Having a clear image in our minds of what we are trying to become is motivating and keeps us focused on what we need to do. A personal vision is a long-term goal that guides our learning. It might not be reached, but that is not as important as having a self-development north star that we can follow. Develop a personal vision for yourself, and help staff and volunteers develop their own personal learning visions. This vision should be aligned with the vision of your organization. For example, your vision might be to provide service to customers that exceeds their expectations, whereas your organization's vision might be to become the provider of choice in your community. Your personal vision serves the organization's vision. That's the kind of alignment that will contribute to building an effective organization.

Individualized Learning Plans

Help staff develop individualized learning plans. These plans are very specific commitments to learning and performance. Learning plans can take many different forms, but essentially, they are statements about the knowledge, skills, attitudes, and beliefs that staff intend to learn; how this learning will be applied on the job to achieve organizational goals; when this will be done; and how the organization will know that performance improvement has occurred. The plan should be tailored to the different learning styles and work contexts of each employee.

Gilley, Boughton, and Maycunich (1999) describe five steps in the creation of an individualized learning plan:

Step 1: Identifying performance objectives

Step 2: Identifying learning resources and strategies

Step 3: Creating transfer of learning strategies

Step 4: Identifying target dates for completion of each performance objective

Step 5: Measuring performance enhancement and improvement

Following these five steps will create a plan that is individualized and practical, and has accountability. The learner will know what he or she needs to learn for the benefit of the organization, how that learning will be applied in the organization, and how the organization will know if there has been a change that contributes to organizational learning.

Self-Reflection

Structure time for your own reflection. Select an experience from which you want to learn, such as leadership of a team meeting, a presentation to a group, a performance review with an employee, or a small group work session. Use Tool 4.1 to ask yourself reflective questions about those activities, and discuss your answers with your supervisor, your learning partner, or your team.

Logs, Diaries, and Journals

Record your reflections and learning in a log, diary, or journal. After repeating this exercise for three or more events, you will discover yourself being more insightful about learning during any experience.

Tool 4.1	Self-Reflection Worksheet

Have I had any new ideas from this experience?

Which ideas stand out as being most important to me?

How do these ideas relate to other ideas I know about?

How can I use these ideas in my work?

How did I react to the discussion in these activities?

How did I relate (positively and negatively) to other people in the activity? What might have caused me to relate in that way?

When during the activity did I feel my interest rising? Declining? What might have caused these shifts in my interest?

What was it about the experience that made it easy for me to learn? What made it difficult? What does that say about how I prefer to learn?

What do I plan to do as a result of what I have learned from this experience?

SOURCE: Adapted from Using Reflection to Leverage Learning by Marilyn W. Daudelin & D. T. Hall in *Training & Development*, December 1997, pp. 13–14.

Also, the act of recording your reflections in a log as they occur will become second nature to you. Although in the rush of your work life you will always benefit from setting aside time dedicated to reflection, you will find yourself thinking of log entries from all kinds of day-to-day experiences if you structure this activity into your schedule.

This activity should be supported by organization culture. This happens when keeping a log, diary, or journal is considered part of the workday and is encouraged by management. It should be recognized as part of the mix of learning methods used by employees and volunteers in the organization.

Job Rotation

Periodically changing jobs within the organization can give you or the people you supervise an eye-opening learning experience. This is especially true if the jobs are in different departments that are suppliers and customers of each other. You will end up learning about work processes from different perspectives. For example, spending some time in operations, accounting, development, program planning, human resources, and volunteer services will help you understand how these departments can work together to meet the needs of external customers and achieve the goals of your nonprofit.

However, to maximize learning, you must be clear about the learning goals. You must know what you are intending to learn from each job in the rotation. Your individualized learning plan should include objectives and how you will know when these objectives have been achieved. Plan reflection time for yourself and for receiving feedback from your supervisor, coworkers, and subordinates.

Individual Coaching

Individual coaching is a learning relationship between two people. This could be you coaching someone you supervise, you coaching another manager, or you could be coached by a coworker or external executive coach. The process is focused on a specific learning need, a performance deficit, a problem among staff and volunteers, or a career goal. Coaching is the process of facilitating self-awareness, learning, and performance improvement of staff or volunteers, often on the job.

Actually, coaching is more than a method. Coaching is a way of being with another person. It is listening, asking, and speaking that draws out and augments characteristics and potential that are already present in a person (Gallwey, 2000). An effective coaching relationship creates a safe and challenging environment in which learning can take place. As with mentoring, listening without judgment is the basis of creating an effective coaching relationship and facilitating learning. Here are some suggestions for listening effectively:

1. Stop talking to yourself (as in, trying to create an argument in your mind for a particular position you want to take with the person you are coaching). You can't listen if you are talking.

2. Put yourself in the other person's shoes. Imagine yourself in her position, doing her work, facing her problems, using her language, and having her values. Ask yourself: What must she be feeling about the situation?

3. Look, act, and be interested. Show your interest through your body language and your verbal responses.

4. Observe nonverbal behavior, like body language, to glean meanings beyond what is said to you.

5. Don't interrupt unless a short interruption can be used to clarify what the employee is saying to you.

6. Listen between the lines for implicit meanings as well as explicit ones.

7. Speak only affirmatively, with short comments, while listening. Resist the temptation to jump in with an evaluative remark, for example: "that's a good thing to do"; "that is against policy"; or "I don't agree."

8. Rephrase what the other person has just told you at key points (when the person has finished speaking about one idea or experience) in the conversation.

9. Stop talking (this is the first and last suggestion because all other techniques of listening depend on you doing this). (Adapted from Senge, Kleiner, Roberts, Ross, & Smith, 1994, p. 391)

As a coach, you are creating a partnership that puts the focus on staff or volunteer learning as opposed to your teaching (Cory & Bradley, 1998). Your job is to support the learning and performance of another person. You do this by asking questions and giving feedback in a manner that is nonthreatening and nonjudgmental to the person being coached. This prevents the defensive thoughts and feelings that people tend to have that usually get in the way of their learning. The way to have a coaching conversation about an event is to follow these four steps:

Step 1: Ask the person what worked well for him or her during the activity (the meeting, the conversation, the presentation, etc.) and why he or she thinks it worked well.

Step 2: Ask what didn't work well for him or her and why he or she thinks it did not work well.

Step 3: Ask what he or she might consider doing differently next time.

Step 4: Offer any feedback you might have from your perspective. Start with what worked, and then describe the behaviors you observed that didn't work and options for change.

As a coach, it is your job to reduce or eliminate obstacles to learning. One of the key obstacles is perception of one's own capability and how that capability appears to others. Employees and volunteers are often stymied in their learning because they

- want to appear competent and knowledgeable
- assume that the need to learn indicates a deficiency
- fear being judged
- have self-doubt about being able to perform up to the expectations of coworkers
- try too hard to learn

Coaching is intended to help "clients" get past this self-doubt. The focus of the coach is on eliciting ideas and solutions from the "coachee," not on telling the employee what is right and wrong (which is common practice by supervisors in the workplace).

You might have a coaching discussion with a staff member while he or she is practicing or actually trying to apply new knowledge or skills. But more often, the coaching occurs on the fly and not while staff are applying what they have learned. A delay occurs between the coaching session and application of learning. In these situations, you will have to coach "retrospectively" by asking questions that help the person relive the event.

Coaching should always provide an opportunity for learning. Be sure to reinforce the new, positive behavior by praising the person immediately when you see the desired action (for example, saying something as simple as, "Good job!"). Your supervisee is more likely to continue this more positive behavior when he or she feels recognized and appreciated for the change.

Career coaching is a little different from performance coaching, but it, too, is an opportunity for learning. This kind of coaching involves helping people match their interests, abilities, and life situations with jobs in the organization and, in some cases, with jobs outside of the organization. The purpose is to develop a good job fit that brings success to the individual and contributes to a successful organization. If that can be done within your organization, that's great. If not, it's better for the learner, the organization, and the community for the person to move to something in another organization that is a better fit.

Mentoring

Mentoring is a relationship between a mentor, who is someone with greater experience and expertise, and a mentee, who is the person being mentored, for the purpose of personal and professional development. Less structured than coaching, mentoring depends on the mentor and mentee forming a learning partnership in which the employee learns from the expertise and experience of the senior person. The mentor must be able to counsel, guide, and teach in a way that is helpful to the learner. The mentor and mentee must be able to develop a relationship of mutual respect. Although the mentee is the identified learner in this relationship, both will learn when mentoring is done well.

Mentors can provide immediate and tailored learning opportunities for staff. This is especially helpful with new employees at all levels in the organization. These employees are trying to figure out their role, how they can contribute, how to relate effectively to their coworkers and supervisors, and how to gain the respect of others. They need a relationship with someone who can provide this guidance.

If you want to be an effective mentor, you must learn to listen. Not just hear, listen! By this I mean putting aside our tendency to judge others, to try to sell an idea to the person, or to advocate for a particular belief or position. Any of these tactics will simply put up a psychological barrier between you and the person you are trying to help. Try to understand staff from their point of view. See suggestions for listening effectively in the section above on coaching.

In most instances, you should not be a mentor to your direct reports. Your supervisory relationship with them can conflict with the mentoring role. This does not usually create the conditions for a good mentoring relationship.

Once you understand a mentee's problems or needs, then share any useful information or related experiences you have had that will help that person learn from the situations. Maybe learning the ropes in the new organization was hard for you, but you figured out some actions you could take that would be useful to your mentee. Maybe you learned what works and what does not work when building a core team for a new project and you could pass that along to your mentee. The mentee's situation will be different from your situation, but together you can decide what can be learned from your experiences.

Mentoring is more art than science. A step-by-step structure does not usually fit. The quality of the mentor-mentee relationship is the key.

Blue Cross and Blue Shield of North Carolina (BCBSNC) has been recognized for its mentoring program ("Best Practices," 2004). This program was designed to "identify high-potential employees, develop talent, enhance cross-functional relationships and create networking opportunities" (p. 62). Mentors go through a rigorous training program and make a commitment of 9 months. A steering committee guides the program. Mentees apply, are selected, and then paired with a trained mentor. BCBSNC attributes a decrease in turnover, cost avoidance, and performance improvements to its mentoring program. What makes this program unusual among mentoring efforts in organizations is that it is strategic. That is, it is designed to achieve specific learning and performance improvement goals that will increase organizational effectiveness.

Computer Technology

You have a growing opportunity to use electronic tools for satisfying many of the learning needs of individual staff and volunteers. I do not mean using the tools to deliver instructor-centered training faster and cheaper, which was typical of this technology when first introduced. I mean using the technology to facilitate just-in-time learning, put learners in control of their own learning, and maintain and continually enhance that learning over time.

If you are a large enough nonprofit to have information technology and training units, work with your information technology and systems staff, your process design staff, and the training staff to develop an integrated electronic performance support system (Gery, 1991). This is a system of online tools that helps people learn when and where they need to learn in order to enhance their immediate performance on the job.

Some of the electronic options include the following:

- Conferencing—link people in different locations at the same time for a learning event.
- Computer-based training—use a personal computer for synchronous (at the same time as the instructor) or asynchronous (at the convenience of the learner) instruction; the Internet or your organization's intranet can be used for delivery of this option.
- Network information—provide online information needed to build the capacity of the learner; use the organization's computer network to do this. This could be in the form of a wiki or weblog that allows everyone in the organization to contribute to and shape the content.
- Computer-supported collaborative work—use networked computers equipped with common operating systems and software for collaborative work among learners.

The possibilities are expanding every day. Team members, although separated by thousands of miles, participate in virtual meetings and work on projects together. An employee forgets how to fill out the new purchase order form, hits a key on her computer, and an online tool appears on the screen that guides her through the task. After employees return from a week-long leadership development workshop, a window appears on their computer screens when they log on each day. In this window is additional information related to the workshop and information that reinforces learning from the workshop.

On-the-Job Training

Structured on-the-job training (OJT) is the planned process of developing task-level expertise by having experienced staff train novice staff at or near the actual work setting (Jacobs & Jones, 1995). A study for the American Society for Training and Development and the U.S. Department of Labor estimated that 80% to 90% of an employee's job knowledge and skills are learned on the job (Carnevale & Gainer, 1989). Think about it. After an initial orientation program (if there is one), where do most staff, whether working directly with clients in the field or doing administrative work from an office, learn how to perform the day-to-day activities of their jobs? Usually, this learning occurs at their workplace, from their coworkers, through direct instruction, or by observing what others do. If you neglect this on-the-job process, you will be missing a prime opportunity for facilitating staff learning and you will be leaving to serendipity the development of knowledge, skills, attitudes, and beliefs that people need to help the organization reach its potential.

All employees and volunteers must perform certain job tasks, such as solving problems, making decisions, inspecting services, following procedures, planning and organizing resources, and using tools. You can help staff learn to perform these tasks by planning and executing OJT. Although this process will be somewhat different depending on whether the training needed is managerial, technical, or awareness (informational or motivational), follow these generic steps:

1. Prepare the learner—topics could include purpose of training, prerequisites, requirements, process of training, questions from learner

2. Present the training—topics could include overview of task, examples, parts of task, demonstration, desired outcomes of task, summary

3. Require a response—steps could include learner describes task, learner demonstrates task, learner summarizes learning

4. Provide feedback—using coaching

5. Evaluate performance—compare to standards and desired outcomes

Tools for Individual Learning

Effective individual learning in your organization depends on feedback and self-reflection. Use the following tools to gather this feedback and structure the reflection process. Essentially, this is linking individual learning to organizational goals.

Use the checklist in Tool 4.2 as a guide for your support of learning before, during, and after a learning event. This can be useful to you in your coaching of others and as a supervisor. Before staff or

---

Tool 4.2 **Checklist for Individual Learning**

Make a checkmark next to each thing you have completed.

Before learning events, help individuals

_____ Understand how their performance must change to help the organization meet its goals
_____ Understand the goals and objectives of the event
_____ Have reasonable expectations for their own performance during and after the learning event
_____ Arrange an opportunity to apply the new knowledge, skills, beliefs, and attitudes immediately after the event
_____ Be aware of your support and encouragement for their learning and performance improvement

During the learning events, help individuals

_____ Understand what they will have to do to apply the new knowledge, skills, beliefs, and attitudes to their work
_____ Explain what they are learning to others
_____ Practice the skills taught during the event
_____ Receive feedback on their knowledge and skills
_____ Be prepared for any obstacles in the workplace that might interfere with their performance of the new skills
_____ Feel the support and encouragement that you have for their learning and performance improvement

After events, help individuals

_____ Apply the new knowledge, skills, beliefs, and attitudes to their work
_____ Receive rewards for learning and application to their work
_____ Remove any obstacles to applying the learning
_____ Receive feedback on how well they are performing
_____ Understand additional learning needs and how to meet these needs
_____ Understand how their continuous learning will help the organization achieve its goals
_____ Feel the support and encouragement that you have for their learning and performance improvement

volunteers attend a workshop, conference, Web-based course, or some other event designed for learning, ask them to go through this list together and help them do as much of it as possible. Think about what else you could be doing to support individual learning.

Use the Learning Process Planning Chart (Tool 4.3) with staff and volunteers prior to the learning event to decide what can be done before, during, and after the event to maximize the impact of learning.

Tool 4.3   Learning Process Planning Chart

Think of an employee or volunteer and what that person needs to learn to be more effective. Then, think of a learning event that might facilitate this learning, such as a workshop, seminar, computer-based course, videotape, audiotape, or reading material such as an article or book. Fill in the following planning tool. What should happen before, during, and after the learning event to ensure that learning occurs and that the new knowledge, skills, attitudes, and beliefs are retained and applied to achieve organizational success?

Discuss this chart with the learner. What will you do to enhance each phase of the learning process? For example, you might discuss your joint expectations for learning outcomes and how they are linked to your nonprofit's performance goals. During the time of the learning event, you might ask the learner to report to you how the event is enhancing his or her capacity to help the organization be successful. After the event, you might discuss how the new knowledge is being applied in the workplace. This tool can also be applied to less structured learning processes, such as coaching and mentoring, in the same way. Here is an example of a completed chart for learning about fundraising.

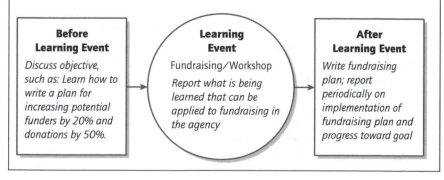

Fill in the spaces provided. Insert what you will do to prepare them for learning; what you will do to ensure they are getting the most out of the event, especially if it is multiday event; and what you will do after the event to support their application of learning. Ask them to insert what they intend to achieve from the event, how they will participate, and how they intend to apply their learning after the event. Have regular conversations with learners throughout the learning process to monitor progress and assess results. This is a powerful way to leverage learning events for the benefit of the organization.

Summary

Individual learning is the first level of organizational learning. Individuals are constantly being exposed to opportunities to learn and build their own capacity to help the organization be successful. These opportunities can be highly structured, such as workshops and seminars, or they can be informal, such as the activities and interactions in the normal course of work. In either case, reflective inquiry is the critical process for learning in organizations. It is the process of asking questions that generate feedback from others or from your own observations and then using this information to continually improve. As an individual, learning how to learn from reflective inquiry will build one's capacity to continually improve performance and will contribute to a culture of learning across the organization.

Individual learning becomes team learning when the collective learning of individuals contributes to organizational performance. For example, managers in a nonprofit attend a course and read books on being mission driven. They learn individually about clarity of purpose; the engagement of staff and board members; and use of the mission statement in planning, budgeting, marketing, and fundraising. As individuals, they become better informed and might even work on a mission statement for themselves or their departments. This learning becomes collective learning when groups of employees and volunteers are able to create a mission statement collaboratively, when groups are able to make joint decisions about new programs that are aligned with the organization's mission, and when the whole board is able to make policy decisions effectively based on the priorities dictated by the mission. The next chapter is an examination of this collective learning in teams.

5

Team Learning

The meeting of two personalities is like the contact of two chemical substances: if there is any reaction, both are transformed.

—Carl Jung

Team learning is the second level of organizational learning. Team learning means leveraging collective knowledge and wisdom of a small group of people. This level of learning, when it is occurring in multiple teams in a nonprofit, contributes to a learning culture that builds the capacity of that organization to successfully design and implement effective projects and programs. If given the opportunity and direction, teams make better decisions than individuals. They do not necessarily make faster decisions, just better decisions. The combined knowledge of group members and the diversity of their opinions and viewpoints allow decisions to be informed by the full complexity of an organization. This observation has been supported by research over and over again.

This chapter makes the case for supporting teams and team learning in nonprofits. I make the distinction between teams and work groups and explain how learning contributes to well-functioning teams and how well-functioning teams contribute to learning.

Work Group Versus Team

Much lip service is being given to teamwork these days, and just about any time two or more coworkers serve on a committee together, or are assigned to the same project, or work in close proximity, they are labeled a "team." However, to achieve organizational success, nonprofits must develop work groups into teams. Work groups are simply collections of individuals who work in close proximity and on closely related tasks. On the other hand, a team is

> a small number of people with complementary skills who are committed to a common purpose, performance goals, and approach for which they hold themselves mutually accountable. (Katzenbach & Smith, 1993, p. 45)

In a learning culture, well-functioning teams have members who learn together and learn how to learn together. Team members help each other achieve a common purpose and hold each other accountable for doing so. If a team's purpose is to feed homeless families, then team members help each other collect, prepare, and distribute food and communicate the expectation that everyone on the team will contribute in some way to achieving this goal. Any gaps in their resources (people's time, food, facilities, etc.) will be filled by members of the team. As they do this task, they learn how to be an effective team; that is, how to work together, learn from each other, improve their work, and succeed.

Both work groups and teams are opportunities for learning. However, there is a difference. The more powerful structure for learning is the true team. Teams are dependent on organizational learning for their success. Learning in a team is "a continuous process by which team members acquire knowledge about the larger organization, the team, and the individual team members" (Russ-Eft et al., 1997, p. 139). But whether staff are working together simply because they share the same task (work group) or they are together because their success is determined by their ability to function as a cohesive, coordinated, integrated unit (team), both types of groups can learn.

Group-focused organizational learning enhances the capacity of a small group (approximately 2 to 20 people) to act as a unit in the workplace. The members' collective "know-how" and "know-why"

(Kim, 1993a) change the culture, behavior, and effectiveness of the group. Group members are both learning together and learning how to learn together.

Losada (1999) has demonstrated the power of "connectivity" in creating high-functioning teams. Connectivity, defined by the number and quality of interactions among group members, is what creates this environment and makes high-performance groups successful. Connectivity is achieved by balancing inquiry (asking questions out of interest in other people's ideas) with advocacy (selling your own ideas), balancing a focus on others (asking about or commenting on another person) with a focus on oneself (making "I" statements and talking about oneself), and maintaining a high ratio of positive feedback (showing appreciation and encouragement of others) to negative feedback (showing disapproval, sarcasm, or cynicism). Losada found in his research that teams with high levels of connectivity were more successful than those with low levels of connectivity. Inquiry, focus on others, and positive feedback, in balance, are all necessary for creating an environment in which participants are receptive to new ideas and feedback.

A high-performance team will discover through its own experience how to become a more effective part of the system. This learning builds the capacity of the group to achieve high performance and to help the organization achieve its potential.

A local United Way organization might have several separate but interdependent teams working at the same time. One team might be working on increasing corporation involvement in the annual campaign; another might be planning the startup of a health and human services information clearinghouse; and a third might be working on an end-of-annual-campaign event to recognize major donors and volunteers who served on allocation committees. Each of these teams, by reflecting on the way the members work together, can learn effective teamwork. The organization as a whole, by taking stock of how all of the teams work together, can learn about supporting the work of the teams and integrating each of the teams into the whole.

Team Development

Teams that achieve high performance in the workplace go through a process of learning and change that causes them to become increasingly effective. The Drexler/Sibbet Team Performance Model (Drexler, Sibbet, & Forrester, 1988) is a good tool for keeping in mind the stages of team development that make up this process and the learning that needs to happen at each stage. These stages are not necessarily linear. For example, goal and role clarification (Stage 3) might occur while trust building (Stage 2) is still going on. Below is an explanation of the Team Performance Model stages.

Stages of the Drexler/Sibbet Team Performance Model

Stage 1: Orientation

Group members need to understand why they are in the group and why others are there. They need to know how they can contribute to the work of the team. They need to believe that the team can accomplish something worthwhile.

Stage 2: Trust Building

Group members need to be able to trust the other members of the team and need to feel trusted by them. When team members trust each other, the feedback is more open and honest. Members learn that their own risk taking builds this trust.

Stage 3: Goal/Role Clarification

Group members need to know the specific task of the group—what is within its charge and what is outside its charge—and what each person's responsibilities are with respect to those goals. Consensus on the purpose of the group and roles of members must be reached before meaningful work can be done.

Stage 4: Commitment

Group members need to know how they will do their work together. They need to have a shared understanding of how decisions will be made; how resources will be used; and, probably most importantly, how dependent they are on each other to achieve the group goals.

Stage 5: Implementation

Group members need to have a clear picture in their minds of the overall process for achieving the team goals. They need to understand how their role and responsibilities fit into this picture and that what they are doing is aligned with what everyone else on the team is doing.

Stage 6: High Performance

Not all teams achieve high performance; only those teams that become highly interdependent, highly interdisciplinary, and creative. This is a transitory state of harmony, order, and flexibility when all team members are working in unison toward team goals.

Stage 7: Renewal

From time to time in the life of a team, members must decide to either recommit themselves to the work of the group or no longer continue as a team. This decision is either rejuvenating to a group that still has value to its members or freeing to members who have ceased to find value in the work.

Reflective Inquiry

As with individual learning, reflective inquiry is critical to learning in teams. Reflective inquiry surfaces evidence of process and results. This creates awareness among team members of their progress and accomplishments. Through this process of questioning and thoughtful self-examination, a mirror is put up in front of the group. Members can say if they like what they see or if they want to change what they see. Without this reflection, it is difficult for teams to learn.

In the workload and time pressures of their day-to-day lives, teams often form and disband and form again without ever reflecting on their own performance and learning. "It would be nice, but we don't have time to do that," is the usual refrain. But if you want to build a culture of learning, you must integrate reflective inquiry into the work processes of your teams. They must make opportunities for feedback and deliberation on the meaning of that feedback. They must continually take stock of their progress, assess their performance, examine what they have accomplished in comparison to the organization's goals, and create awareness of the learning that has occurred.

Examine your teams in terms of the Drexler/Sibbett Team Performance Model of stages of team development. Look for signs that a team is moving through each stage and achieving the learning that needs to occur to make progress toward high performance. Provide feedback to teams so that they can learn and improve. Remind team members of the work that needs to be done to fully develop as a team, and that this is sometimes a long and bumpy road.

Team Learning Methods

A selection of methods that incorporate reflective inquiry in teams is described below. To have maximum effect, each of these methods must be tailored to the needs of a particular group. The team members should work together to agree to goals and performance outcomes for each activity. In other words, ask, "What do we want our team to learn from this experience, and how should this learning be applied on the job?"

Shared Vision

Managing by shared vision is much more productive than managing by coercion or by command and control. Creating a shared vision is the process of achieving consensus on the direction of the group and on the desired results—that is, everyone on the team having the same goals for the future and being guided by the same underlying principles. A shared vision is the backdrop for learning and change. When staff know where they are trying to get to, they can figure out what they need to learn to be successful in getting there.

For example, 10 employees selected from across a large institution were charged with developing a performance management system for the agency. They began their work together by clarifying their collective vision for the product of the group. Group leaders constantly checked to make sure everyone's thoughts and feelings were being recognized and heard in meetings. Consensus was achieved on a set of values and principles and a conceptual framework for the final product. The group also agreed to the meaning and significance this product would have for the future direction of the organization. By the time this "goal clarification" stage was completed, the group had become a team. They shared a vision for the product and for how they would continue to work together, both during formal meetings and outside of scheduled meetings. They learned how to fill the roles that were needed in making this process successful. Without any directives from the identified leader, group members taught each other whatever they could to help the group in its work, initiated efforts outside of meetings to support specific tasks, and applied group process facilitation skills that they learned in the meetings. They learned about performance management, but even more important, they learned how to learn in a group. They created a learning culture for themselves and, in the long run, this is what will build the capacity of the organization to be successful.

Work as a total team to develop a shared vision. Do not try to impose a vision from the top of the organization. Although top management's endorsement and financial support for the vision is important, team ownership of the vision will not occur when that vision is promulgated exclusively by top management. Employees will not feel like the vision belongs to them unless they have a say in creating it. They will not understand the reasons for organizational change or performance improvement unless they know the facts. They will not be motivated to learn unless they believe in the new direction for the organization. Provide opportunities for all group members to have input and share reactions to that input among each other.

If some team members have a vision for the team that is not shared by others (for example, they are using it as a vehicle for their own recognition and promotion), they will not contribute to team learning. The group energy will be scattered like a searchlight over a large and diffuse area. Each member will be focused on his or her own personal situation and not that of the team. However, if everyone in the group is committed to the same long-term goals, then, like a laser beam, the energy will be concentrated on a single target that keeps everyone working and learning together.

This does not mean that everyone on the team must do the same thing or even approach the problem in the same way. In fact, having a shared vision frees up group members to try new approaches to the problem. For example, team members in one human services nonprofit had a shared vision that there would be shelter for all individuals and families in need of temporary housing. Some team members contributed by working on securing local housing options, others worked on collecting food and clothing, others worked on employment opportunities for those homeless individuals who were able to work, and still others worked on housing policies that affected homeless individuals and families. Everyone worked in his or her own way toward the shared vision.

A shared vision is created from a process that builds group consensus for its elements and builds a sense of ownership (a belief in personal responsibility for how results are achieved) in the goals. One method for developing consensus and ownership is holding a visioning meeting of group members.

A typical visioning session has at its core the following elements:

1. Presentation of background information about the organization, its history, its current status, the environment in which it functions, and its strategic goals

2. Consensus on what the team does well, in what activities it has been successful, and what resources it has available for the future

3. Consensus on the principles that guide the work of the team

4. Discussion of how this picture of the team fits with the vision for the organization as a whole

5. Brainstorming of what team members would like to see the team achieve in 3, 5, or 10 years

6. Consensus on the top priority items from the brainstorm list

7. Discussion and listing of the implications for the team of working toward these goals

8. Identification of what the team needs to learn how to do and what knowledge it needs to have in order to achieve these goals

Sustaining a shared vision over time requires continual maintenance. As the months and years go by, events, developments, and trends in the environment will require you to change your vision. As staff learn and change and the makeup of the team changes, the group may lose sight of or be less committed to the principles and goals. For example, it is relatively easy to commit to outstanding customer service when the budget is balanced and you are fully staffed. This goal is more difficult to sustain, but even more critical, when funds are down and staff are working harder than ever. Find ways to remind team members of the vision and periodically repeat the visioning process, or at least give staff an opportunity to either affirm their commitment to the current vision or work on creating a new vision for the team.

Action Learning

Action learning is learning from doing. It is evaluative inquiry in action. It is intentionally engaging a team in a work activity for the purpose of learning and change, having group members reflect on the process and outcomes of that activity, and then using that newfound awareness for improving performance.

What we do is often inconsistent with the values that we say we believe in.[1] We are often not aware of this inconsistency. Action learning gives us an opportunity to surface our behavior in relation to the group and surface the values underlying this behavior. For example, a manager who says he believes that all employees deserve respect and trust might be doing things that are inconsistent with this value, such as creating rules and expressing expectations that are different for different employees. He might encourage John to meet with prospective donors by himself, but always asks Sally to team up with a coworker when she goes to see a new donor. The manager might have a good reason for this difference, but it is not readily apparent and quickly gets interpreted as sexism by staff. The result of not being aware of this inconsistency is the inadvertent concealment of problems, leading to confusion, frustration, and possibly distrust in others. The manager should be using "after-action learning" to inquire about his actions and reflect on the meaning of what others say about those actions.

Three kinds of group-focused action learning lead to group learning: (a) reflection-on-action (looking back on what happened), (b) reflection-in-action (examining the situation while you are in it), and (c) reflection-for-action (focusing on what was learned and how that learning can be used in the future) (Schön, 1983). Questions that can guide each kind of team reflection are listed below. Ask these questions of your team whenever you want to learn from a project or event on which you have worked or are currently working on together.

Reflection-on-action:

- How does the group feel about the situation?
- What went well?
- What did not go as well as we expected?
- What options did we consider as we selected the behavior/action?
- What option did we choose?
- How did we know that what we chose to do was best in this situation? On what did we base that decision (e.g., theory, experience, intuition)?
- How did we know that another behavior/action would not be appropriate?
- What made this situation unusual?
- What might we have done differently?

Reflection-in-action:

- What cues from the group do we see that tell us how they are responding to our behaviors/actions?
- What assumptions or inferences are we making?
- What options are available? What are the possible consequences of each? What would work best in this situation?
- What principles/theories are guiding us?
- What is unique about this situation?
- What level of direction/specificity/structure is best here?

Reflection-for-action:

- What did we learn that we can apply in other situations?
- How did we alter our knowledge, theories, or attitudes as a result of this experience?
- What did we learn from this situation that confirms our expectations?
- What will we remember from this situation?
- If we were in a similar situation again, how would we behave?

Create situations from which you think you can learn. For example, at the next team meeting you are leading, make it a point to learn about your own meeting leadership behavior. Or, in the next team project, learn about your project management behavior. Or, in the next performance review discussion you have with someone you supervise, ask for feedback about your coaching skills. You may want a peer to sit in on the session, observe, and then provide the feedback rather than asking the person you are coaching to do this. Use the Self-Directed Action Learning Worksheet (Tool 5.2).

Action learning is not just another discussion group. A learning environment must be created where members feel safe to talk about their experiences, "warts and all," to learn from mistakes, rather than feeling like they have to explain or give an excuse for their actions. Team members should listen to the experiences of others and offer careful and constructive support by asking challenging questions. And then they should support and recognize changes in individual and group behavior that occur as a result of that action learning.

Continuous Measurement

Learning in teams is enhanced by continuous measurement. By measurement I mean surfacing and collecting data that indicate the performance quality of the team. Data can be numbers or narrative or both, as long as they are credible evidence to team members and other stakeholders. These data are used to evaluate progress and outcomes. The data keep the team focused on progress toward goals and keep members energized. Teams that do not receive this kind of feedback will stagnate and lose energy. Tool 5.1 provides questions that your team can ask itself to surface evaluative data.

The method you should use for measurement depends on which of these questions you are asking. The most common method for assessing team members' attitudes, perceptions, and self-report of behavior is a survey. However, for other kinds of questions, there are other, more effective methods. These include the following:

- Individual, face-to-face interviews of team members and people who interact with the team
- Group interviews of all team members
- Structured observations of team meetings
- Surveys of the team's internal and external customers
- Telephone or computer-aided interviews of team members
- Analysis of performance indicators as reported in the organization's records

The data gathering should be appropriate to the situation and to collecting and reporting the kind of information needed by the particular team for continuous improvement or accountability. For example, if you want to find out member attitudes toward being on the

Tool 5.1	Questions for Continuous Measurement of Team Performance

Use these questions to drive continuous measurement of your own team. Ask yourselves:

1. What are our learning and performance goals as a group?

2. Does our team have the right people and skills to achieve our goals?

3. What will we have to learn in order to be successful?

4. Does our meeting structure encourage honest interaction and cooperation?

5. Do we feel mutually respected and trusted?

6. Do we believe that we can take risks and make mistakes without penalty?

7. Are we receiving the recognition and reward that we deserve?

8. What are we learning?

9. To what extent is our team making progress toward our performance goals?

10. What is it about the structure and culture of the larger organization that facilitates our team's learning and development?

11. What is it about the structure and culture of the larger organization that is a barrier to our team's learning and development?

12. What must be changed for us to be more effective as a team? How might we create this change?

13. What have we accomplished as a team?

14. How has our team affected the larger organization?

15. How has our team contributed to the larger organization achieving its strategic goals?

16. What additional questions would you like to investigate about our team? List them here.

_____

_____

_____

_____

team, then interview or survey team members. If you want to know about progress in team development (e.g., team formation, communication among members, meeting dynamics, problem solving and decision making, rewards and recognition), observe the team in action and compare your observations to the observations of other team leaders and team members. If you want to know the impact of the team on the organization, survey the internal customers and examine indicators of team output. But collect only data that you and others will use to improve practice. To do otherwise is to waste time and resources and threaten the credibility of your relationship with team members.

The real value of continuous assessment of teams is in using the findings to enhance the capacity of the team to be successful and increase the impact on the larger organization. Your role is to

- help teams participate in, understand, and value the continuous measurement process. Engage team members as much as possible in collecting and interpreting data.
- help teams learn from the data and use the data for planning purposes.
- ask team members: What do the data say about the team's performance? What do the data say about resource needs? How should the team change the way it functions, given the data? How can the team ensure that its goals are met? What information should be communicated to the wider organization?
- help the team learn how to learn from continuous assessment.

Dialogue

Dialogue can be defined as learning through conversation (Bohm, 1996; Isaacs, 1999). The word *dialogue* is often used to mean any kind of serious exchange of ideas. Here, I am using *dialogue* in a special sense. This is a kind of conversation in which you try to understand the other person's point of view rather than convince that person of your point of view. Listen to each other, surface underlying assumptions and beliefs, and weave connections among ideas. You are not looking for solutions at this point. Agreement is not important. What is important is listening to all ideas and opinions and finding clarity in what is meant by what people are saying.

The process requires stepping outside of our typical patterns of behavior in conversations and being open to the thoughts, ideas, and feelings of others. The intent is to achieve shared meaning among all of the participants in the conversation. In its purest form, it is the nature of the interaction within a conversation, rather than the positions people hold about a topic, that is most important.

Dialogue can also be used intentionally in a group to achieve shared meaning about a particular issue or idea. It can be used as a process for finding common ground among people who typically are in conflict with one another. The first step in helping people use dialogue is to help them understand the difference between debate, which is the common approach to conversation, and dialogue, which requires a radical departure from what most of us do normally. Table 5.1 presents this distinction between debate and dialogue.

Table 5.1   Difference Between Debate and Dialogue

Debate	Dialogue
Assuming that there is a right answer, and you have it	Assuming that many people have pieces of the answer and that together they craft a new solution
Combative: participants attempt to prove the other side wrong	Collaborative: participants work together toward common understanding
About winning	About exploring common ground
Listening to find flaws and make counter-arguments	Listening to understand, find meaning and agreement
Defending assumptions as truth	Revealing assumptions for reevaluation
Critiquing the other side's position	Reexamining all positions
Defending one's own views against those of others	Admitting that others' thinking can improve on one's own
Searching for flaws and weaknesses in other positions	Searching for strengths and value in others' positions
Seeking a conclusion or vote that ratifies your position	Discovering new options, not seeking closure

SOURCE: Gerzon, Mark, Mediators Foundation, 3833 N. 57th Street, Boulder, CO 80301 and The Public Conversations Project, National Study Circles Resources, The Common Enterprise (handout).

Daniel Yankelovich (1999) has identified three distinctive features of the thinking and writing about dialogue:

1. *Equality and the absence of coercive influences.* In the context of the dialogue, all participants must be treated equally. What might exist as superior or coercive positions in the workplace and outside of the dialogue should not exist in the dialogue. This is essential for participants to feel free to express themselves; they should not have to screen their comments because of fear of being judged by others or being punished overtly or covertly. During a dialogue session, do not use your position in the organizational hierarchy to try to influence others, and do not let what is said influence decisions about a person outside of the dialogue.

2. *Listening with empathy.* Empathy is trying to understand another person's thoughts and feelings from that person's point of view. Listening requires your total attention to what that person is saying and, even more importantly, to what that person is trying to communicate by what is being said. These are difficult skills to master. It takes much practice, but when active listening and empathy are being employed among participants in a group, the conversation becomes richer and more meaningful.

3. *Bringing assumptions into the open.* Surface the assumptions behind the issue. Do not judge the rightness or wrongness of these assumptions. For example, a group member might admit to believing that the responsibility for making sure that the work of the group gets done resides with the designated team leader. In another setting, you might react to this comment by thinking that the person is irresponsible and shirking her duties by holding this assumption. In a dialogue, your response to her should be one of acceptance and further conversation about the meaning of her belief and what you and others might learn from this perspective.

Listening to the other person is the key to dialogue. You cannot learn from all that another person has to contribute unless you listen fully to what that person is communicating. This means blocking out those conversations we have with ourselves in our heads about what we agree with and what we disagree with, what we like about the person and what we do not like, and how we can convince that person of our position on an issue. In the space that is left after you block out all of these other conversations you have with yourself, ask yourself these questions:

1. What is this person trying to communicate to me?

2. What does he or she really mean by the words?

3. What are the feelings that go with the words?

4. What do I need to ask in order to more fully understand what he or she is saying?

5. Am I making any assumptions about what is being said that I should ask about?

6. How does what he or she is saying connect to what others have said in the group so far?

The following are basic guidelines for applying dialogue in a small group:

- Hear from everyone in the group. Discover what you have in common. Discuss the challenges that are faced by everyone in the group.
- Recognize that the knowledge and experience that everyone has is sufficient to explore the question.
- Create a spirit of inquiry. Stimulate curiosity and questioning.
- Acknowledge that it is normal to feel both comfort and discomfort in reaction to what others say.
- Accept that no one has the right answer.
- Do not try to prove or persuade. Offer your perspective and look for connections to what others have said.

Learning History

Learning histories are like highly structured group reflections. They provide an opportunity to look back on an important event or series of events in the life of the group and learn collectively from successes and failures (Kleiner & Roth, 1997). The focus could be the history of how a team planned a new program, the history of a major change effort such as changing the mission of a department, or the history of the budget planning process.

The key stakeholders (team members and others who are affected by the work of the team) in the event are interviewed regarding the facts of the event and their reactions and actions in response to the facts of the event. Typically, these interviews are put in the form of a written narrative. The narrative has two columns. The right-hand column contains the story as told by the people who were interviewed, using direct quotes as much as possible. The left-hand column contains an analysis by a group of "learning historians." These can be people within or external to the organization but who are not part of the team. Their job is to identify organizing themes in the content, comment on the meaning of what was said in the right-hand column, pose questions for the reader to consider, and surface undiscussable issues suggested by the story.

In Table 5.2, three managers struggle with their leadership roles in an organization that is changing from autocratic leadership to a democratic decision-making environment. This organization is trying to engage employees in decision making and build a sense of ownership in decisions at all levels. The three leaders are learning what and how they need to change.

To create a learning history, bring coworkers together for a reflective conversation. You may want a facilitator to lead this so that you can join in the group conversation. This facilitator should interview participants beforehand to create a learning history that is a composite of the perceptions of the interviewees. Then, this story becomes the focus of group reflection. The group should examine its values and beliefs in comparison to its actual behavior. New insights will come from this kind of reflective session.

Meeting Management

Teams do much of their work in meetings. Meetings have the potential to be powerful team learning experiences. However, in order for that to happen, these meetings must be designed for this purpose. They must be intentionally designed for learning. Too many meetings are designed, often unintentionally, to disseminate information, not to achieve learning. These meetings tend to use whatever is the traditional meeting format in that organization. Often, this means that the agenda consists of announcements of events and news about the organization, followed by a report from individuals about what they have been doing or are intending to do, followed by updating the schedule. All of this information is important for team members, but this kind of meeting does not support team learning. If you want a team to develop its capacity to achieve its goals, you must design meetings for this purpose. John Tropman (2003) provides excellent suggestions for designing and managing meetings to achieve your goals. Form follows function . . . in meetings as well as in architecture.

Table 5.2   Example of a Learning History: Leaders Find New Roles

These leaders acknowledge their leadership abilities and responsibilities, yet recognize that because the way decisions have to be made is changing, they have to modify their power behaviors with subordinates. Deep shifts in their own attitudes are the starting point.	
Column A:	*Column B:*
Contains learning historians' summary and analysis of what workers said in Column B	What stakeholders have to say about the event; contains information about their reactions and response.

Learning to share decision making with subordinates is one of the most difficult changes for leaders to make.	**Operations Manager 3:** I know personally just how traumatic it has been for me to make the necessary changes, to take off my old management hat. They literally threw me out of the first meetings of the operation-level teams. I said that I was sitting in on the meetings to help the new teams, but they finally just told me, "We don't want you in here; you're not helping us."
	
	    I knew it, but it was hard to let go because I had the information and the answers for them. To let them develop that themselves was very hard.
	
	Senior Manager 2: As leaders, we were accustomed to making decisions. We had some very, very painful moments while we learned how to act like team members and learned how not to make decisions for others. I was probably the worst of the bunch. In the beginning people would say, "She's never going to be able to do this." I didn't think I was going to be able to do it either.
	
	    There were these 200 people around and they wanted instant answers. Somebody would ask me a question in the hall and I knew immediately what I thought they should do, which was what I would have said to them six months ago. Now, though, I had to say to them, "Let me get with the leadership team and I'll get back to you."

	Operations Manager 3: We put a cross-level, operations/human resources team together to implement the change. As the management-level representatives, we explained that we considered everyone else on the team as peers. It was culture shock for the hourly people, though; they were very uncomfortable with managers as peers.
	A key event happened after several months of meetings. The management-level team members, including myself, had gone off and hammered out a vision for the team effort. When we brought it into the team meeting, one of the hourly guys finally said: "If you really want us on this team, I'll tell you what I think: What you've written is BS. No one is going to believe it . . . it's just management rhetoric."
	We managers looked at each other and realized that we had taken over. That was a breaking point. After that, we rewrote the vision as a whole team and went forward from there.
Sharing information across levels is another behavior change that is important in moving change forward.	**Operations Manager 3:** Managers, including myself, don't always realize that the only difference between ourselves and our employees is the amount of information we control. It's not a difference in intelligence. Given the same information, the teams are going to make the same decisions as would the manager. Teams may take a little longer because their base is not as experienced, but they do make the same decision. The resistance is in the manager letting go, giving them the information, and waiting for the decision.
	In our teams that are really working, the manager has let go and the coaches are really coaching.
Positive encouragement helps people find new meaning and satisfaction in the work they do.	**Senior Manager 1:** It's me providing a vision and getting buy-in from those people, but it isn't just me doing it—I always say I don't do much of anything; I stimulate others.

(Continued)

Table 5.2 (Continued)

	Any meaningful change in an organization requires a vision and expectations, and when things get sketchy, requires us to be persistent with those expectations. I just keep talking about them. It's great to watch people change their behavior patterns and recognize their abilities—abilities they didn't know they had. For instance, I saw people who probably had never seen the inside of a math class stand up in front of a group and talk about statistics.
The personal credibility of the leader assumes more importance during transformation.	**Operations Manager 2:** When you lead people, you do it through personal credibility. You know you're not doing all the work, but you're a critical enough piece of the machine that if you fall out, the whole thing comes to an end. You have to have this unwavering focus and discipline, and you really have to believe in what you're doing.

SOURCE: Example originally provided by Ann Thomas. Table from Gill, Stephen J., *The Manager's Pocket Guide to Organizational Development*, HRD Press, 2000, pp. 75–79.

The value of meeting as a group is that the group interaction contributes to achieving a particular goal (e.g., policy decision, strategy decision, implementation decision, delegation decision, recognition of achievement). Meetings are expensive; they cost time, money, and emotional energy. They are a distraction from other activities. However, when group interaction is necessary for the group to achieve the desired outcome, such as organizational learning and capacity building, then a meeting is an excellent vehicle.

Attend to process and dynamics of group meetings. Even though the focus is on the task of the group (for example, planning a new program, creating a new policy, distributing funds among programs, or recognizing achievements of the team), the Drexler-Sibbet principles still apply. Design the meeting so that all participants are clear about the goals, they understand their role in achieving those goals, they understand their role in the meeting, and they trust that leaders and others will provide a safe environment to talk about sensitive issues. Otherwise, not everyone will participate fully and openly, and the team will not have the information and commitment it needs to make the best decisions. From a capacity-building stand-point, the team will not learn how to work together to make effective decisions.

In Table 5.3 are recommendations for turning your team meetings into effective organizational learning experiences.

A social justice advocacy group of volunteers that met monthly applied these Do's and Don'ts. Approximately 20% of the meeting time was allocated to announcements about events in the community, reports on the advocacy efforts of other organizations, and an update on the work of members of this group. Approximately 80% of the meeting time was allocated to discussing social justice issues at the local, state, or national levels and what the group's response should be to those issues. At every meeting, the goals of the group were reviewed and activities of the organization were examined for their alignment with those goals. People participated in this group because of their concern for social justice. To build people's commitment and willingness to contribute their time, effort, and money, most of the meeting time was intentionally dedicated to this purpose and role. The discussion was structured so that everyone in attendance had a voice in decisions. Administrative decisions, such as budget and scheduling space for events, were handled outside of these meetings. Otherwise, each meeting easily could become focused entirely on administration and fail to meet the expectations and achieve the goals of team members.

One way to facilitate learning in a team is to evaluate a meeting's progress and results, and then use these data for feedback and reflection. This begins with clarity of goals. As soon as you decide what you want to achieve in the meeting and how you want to achieve it, you can begin thinking about evaluation. Write down the questions that you want to ask participants about the meeting. Make sure these questions have a clear relationship to the purposes and goals of the meeting. Ask questions that will provide you with information you can use to improve and plan future meetings.

Table 5.3   How to Turn Your Team Meeting Into an Effective Organizational Learning Experience

DOs	DON'Ts
Do meet to hear everyone's thinking and collect everyone's input on a question, idea, or issue. Encourage everyone on the team to participate. Use group exercises to ensure that this happens, such as a "go-around," where everyone is asked to take a turn responding to questions about the topic.	**Do not** meet just to distribute information, such as news, instructions, policies, upcoming events, and reminders. Use memos, e-mail, faxes, intranet, or a newsletter to do that. The exceptions to this rule are a few very short messages; an announcement that requires a personal touch, such as someone's health status; or announcements that will have an emotional reaction and need your response.
Do meet to decide how to proceed and take action as a team. Use a consensus decision-making process whenever possible. This contributes to building trust and respect among team members and results in a decision that the entire team can support.	**Do not** meet to discipline, give embarrassing feedback, or coach a staff member or volunteer. Doing this in a group will only lead to the individual becoming defensive and not learning. Those actions should be done one-on-one, in private. Otherwise you will threaten the development of trust (Stage 2 of D-S Team Performance Model) in the group.
Do meet to work on learning how to learn in a group. Be explicit about the structure and process of the meeting so that others are clear about what you are doing and why you are doing it. This builds the capacity of the team to continue to plan and execute effective meetings.	**Do not** meet to do something that can be done better individually or in smaller groups. Assign these tasks to be completed outside of the meeting or instead of the meeting.
Do apply action learning principles to observe and learn how to improve the experience of team meetings.	**Do not** meet just because the team has always met at that time and place. Meeting without a clear need to meet foments confusion, uncertainty, and fear (Stage 1 of D-S Team Performance Model). Meetings should be cancelled and rescheduled when necessary.

You might ask participants the following questions:

- Did you understand the purpose of the meeting?
- What was the level of trust that you felt?
- To what extent do you believe that the group's goals can be accomplished?
- Was the decision about working toward the goal made to your satisfaction?
- Is everyone clear about his or her role in achieving the goal?
- What do you think was helpful about the process?
- What do you think should be improved in future meetings?

In addition to asking these questions of the group, ask questions that evaluate your meetings using one or more of the following options:

- Ask evaluation questions orally, for discussion in the group; usually at the end of the meeting.
- Distribute and collect a short questionnaire at the end of the meeting. Summarize the findings, disseminate them to participants, and get their reactions before setting the agenda for the next meeting.
- Conduct a follow-up survey of meeting participants by phone or online. Summarize the findings, disseminate them, and get reactions from participants before setting the agenda for the next meeting.
- Conduct a focus group of a subset of participants immediately following the meeting. Summarize the findings, disseminate them, and get reactions from participants before setting the agenda for the next meeting.
- Arrange for a meeting evaluator to observe the meeting and provide feedback at the end of the meeting or soon after.
- Videotape the meeting and then replay and discuss the meeting with a meeting evaluator.

Team learning depends on collecting feedback about the group, its process for doing its work, and the results, and then using that information for group self-reflection related to performance improvement. This section has provided examples of methods that can be used for collecting this feedback and discussing it with team members. Next, several tools are provided that can be used for this purpose.

Tool 5.2   Self-Directed Action Learning Worksheet

Use this tool to learn from your own and your team's actions in a situation. Use this for learning-for-action, learning-in-action, or learning-from-action. Focus on a particular team task, event, or project. Ask yourself these questions, write down the answers, and then discuss with other team members.

Ask yourself:

1. What do/did I want to learn about myself from this situation?

2. What do/did I want to have happen? What outcome am/was I hoping for?

3. What actually did occur?

4. How did my team members respond to me? What did they say and what did they do?

5. What did I think and say that might have contributed to these outcomes? What assumptions was I making about others?

6. How was what I said or did different from what I had thought I wanted to say and do?

7. How can I get additional feedback on my actions? Who should I ask for reactions and observations?

Tool 5.3	Group Action Learning Worksheet

In practicing action learning in a team, the group should meet to have a conversation about how they are going to deal with some problems or tasks they face in their work. In deciding what to do in these situations, they also increase their understanding of the situations they are in. They learn from each other's experience.

You can help facilitate this conversation by using the group action learning worksheet below.

Ask the group:

1. What did we plan and what assumptions did we make about ourselves, others, and the situation that guided our planning?

2. What happened as we had planned it, and why did this happen?

3. What did not happen as we had planned it, and why did this happen?

4. What did we learn from Questions 2 and 3 above?

5. What did we learn about our assumptions?

6. What was accomplished, and how close was this to our goals?

7. What can we do next time? (Based on what we learned, how can we get results closer to our plan?)

Tool 5.4	Meeting Evaluation Questionnaire

An example of a generic evaluation questionnaire for meetings is the Meeting Evaluation Questionnaire. The purpose for using this questionnaire is to provide participants with a framework for analyzing the effectiveness of a meeting and to explore how the group might improve its meetings in the future.

One way to use this questionnaire is to ask participants to fill it out after a meeting, note the ratings on a scale displayed in front of the group, and then discuss the implications of the group ratings. What improvements are indicated? How can these improvements be achieved? Who will be responsible for each of these improvements?

Instructions: Complete the questionnaire by circling a number at the point on each scale closest to your evaluation of the meeting according to each of the eight criteria.

- Importance

This meeting was of little or no real importance.	This meeting was very important.

1	2	3	4	5	6	7

- Membership

This meeting did not have the right membership for its task.	This meeting had the right membership for its task.

1	2	3	4	5	6	7

- Task

The task of the meeting was unclear.	The task of the meeting was clearly defined.

1	2	3	4	5	6	7

- Climate

The atmosphere in the meeting obstructed progress.	The meeting had a positive, productive atmosphere.

1	2	3	4	5	6	7

- Openness

People felt inhibited or guarded.	People were prepared to speak their minds.

1	2	3	4	5	6	7

• Procedures						
The procedures were often ineffective.				The procedures were generally effective.		
1	2	3	4	5	6	7
• Energy						
Those attending failed to invest much energy in the meeting.				Participation was energetic and stimulating.		
1	2	3	4	5	6	7
• Outside Relationships						
The group integrates poorly with other groups.				The group has constructive relationships with other groups.		
1	2	3	4	5	6	7

SOURCE: This instrument is reproduced from: *The Encyclopedia of Group Activities: 150 Practical Designs for Successful Facilitating*, edited by J. William Pfeiffer, San Diego, CA: University Associates, 1989.

Tool 5.5	Team Competencies Inventory

An effective team has the set of competencies that teams must have to be successful and learn from their experiences. These competencies are developed through individual and team learning experiences. These competencies should not reside in one person. In fact, it is better for team cohesiveness if each team member has at least one of these competencies. Then, it is the collective strength of the individuals that makes the team competent for high performance. Use the following tool to inventory your team's competencies.

Ask your team, "As a team, what competencies do we have, and what do we need to learn?" Go through the list below and make sure that for each of these competencies, at least one member of the team has this capability and has accepted this role in the group. If this competency is lacking in the team, consider seeking outside assistance.

Competency	Name of Team Member
Goal setting	
Meeting agenda setting	
Facilitating meeting process	

(Continued)

Tool 5.5	(Continued)	
Competency	*Name of Team Member*	
Trust building		
Listening and giving feedback		
Problem solving		
Decision making		
Resolving conflict		
Collecting data		
Recording and documenting team actions		
Applying technical and functional expertise		
Training and coaching		
Making presentations		
Assessing team performance		
Planning/managing projects		

Summary

Teams that use evaluative inquiry contribute to a learning culture. These teams are the building blocks of strong and successful organizations, and they offer a rich dynamic for learning and change when they are managed well. Teams are effective when they learn collectively through a process of gathering feedback and then reflect on the implications of that information for performance improvement. This can be done in action or by reviewing in retrospect what happened, why it happened, and what the group can learn from the experience. Keeping this process of learning explicit and apparent to all team members helps them learn how to continuously learn in groups.

Note

1. Argyris and Schön (1974) call this theory-in-use and espoused theory.

6

Whole Organization Learning

You don't get harmony when everybody sings the same note.

—Doug Floyd

This chapter explains how participants in an organization can learn collectively. Whether a three-person advocacy group or a thousand-person international relief organization, effectiveness depends on learning being a collective activity. As Preskill said in her 2007 presidential address to the American Evaluation Association:

> An organization's ability to learn is a critical factor associated not only with survival but also with continued success. As writers on organizational management, change, and development consistently claim, change is the norm, and an organization's future in large part depends on how well it adapts and learns from its employees and the external environment. . . . Consequently, it is widely regarded that the most critical competency for employees is their ability and willingness to learn. (Preskill, 2008, p. 129)

Whole organizations can learn how to manage knowledge, make decisions, solve problems, and change. This learning builds the capacity of a nonprofit to deal with challenges: a changing environment, shifts in resources, new pressures from stakeholders, and its own desire for increased impact. Whole organization learning builds on the individual and team learning described in the previous chapters of this book.

Whole organizations can develop ways of collectively improving the way people work together. They can learn how to create and sustain a community of learners. And they can learn how to learn how to do this.

Learning About Vision

The first thing is for your nonprofit to be clear about its vision and mission. Second is to know how to continue to clarify the organization's vision and mission and how to develop acceptance for that vision and mission throughout the organization. Staff and volunteers should be clear and support the long-term view of what the organization is trying to accomplish, and they should support the products and services that the nonprofit offers its customers. This clarity of direction and purpose is one kind of learning. Learning how to achieve this clarity is another kind of learning. Both are critical for developing an effective organization.

An example of whole organization learning is what happened to a newly formed, statewide organization for providing coordinated services to people with macular degeneration of the eyes. Partner organizations included ophthalmologists, optometrists, researchers, university faculty, staff of professional associations, and companies that produce assistive devices. Partner representatives were brought together for a series of "future search" sessions (Weisbord, 1987). By going through this self-reflection and planning process, they not only created a shared vision for the future of the new organization, they also learned how to work together as a whole organization for ongoing goal setting and strategic planning.

Another example occurred when the leadership of a national professional association, the Financial Planners Association, wanted to bring members together in a different way from the usual format of having an expert lecture at them. They wanted to encourage engaged conversation, giving members an opportunity to talk to each other about issues critical to their profession and the association. They chose the World Café method (see the description of this method later in this chapter). This gave large groups of members an opportunity to speak and listen to each other. The process started a cultural shift in the organization, from a focus on the centralized administration of the association to a focus on its members and their needs (Porto, n.d.).

Having a shared vision helps to give nonprofits cohesion and direction, but it isn't sufficient. Having a systems view, having leaders who are committed to the change necessary to achieve goals, and being willing to stick it out over the long term are important for nonprofits to achieve significant results. These observations are supported by a study of capacity building in nonprofits conducted by McKinsey & Co. with support from Venture Philanthropy Partners. They learned these lessons:

> Effective capacity building . . . is rarely confined to addressing only one of the elements in isolation; as soon as a nonprofit starts digging around in its systems, for example, it invariably discovers that it must also examine, analyze, and address the ramifications that making changes will have on the other elements. For this reason, capacity building must be firmly driven by the senior management of the organization.
>
> In addition, three other lessons emerge that cut across the nonprofit sector, regardless of an organization's size, mission, or business model. The first lesson is that the act of resetting aspirations and strategy is often the first step toward a dramatic improvement of an organization's capacity. Quite simply, unless an organization has a clear idea of its purpose and strategy, it will never reach its full potential. The second lesson is that both leadership and management are important. Nonprofits need people in senior positions who are committed to taking the initiative to make capacity building happen and are willing to "own" it and drive it down through the organization. The third lesson is that you must have patience. In both the nonprofit and for-profit worlds, building capacity can take a long time and can be very frustrating. (McKinsey & Company, 2001, p. 69)

Nonprofit boards play a critical role in setting the overall direction for the organization. Some would argue that all boards should be responsible for the strategic and financial viability of their nonprofit organizations (Carver, 2006; Light, 2001). But many boards do not know how to be strategic or choose not to be strategic, and as a result, they fail to have much impact on the performance of nonprofits. These board members need to learn how to help their organizations answer the strategic questions, "Where to go tomorrow? Who does what? What gets done today? Did it happen?" (Light, 2001, p. vii).

Many nonprofit board members did not sign on for this much responsibility. They joined their boards because of their commitment to a cause, or because of the prestige of being on that board, or because membership on the board provides them with a sense of control and importance that they don't have in other aspects of their lives. Now, faced with having to help the organization change in new and risky ways, board members can become uncomfortable with this level of involvement. Therefore, these board members will need help learning and adjusting to this new role.

Learning to Be Integrative

Whole organization learning depends on an awareness of the inter-dependency of the various units of a nonprofit. Our natural tendency is to analyze—to understand complex entities by separating them into small parts in our thinking and then to make assumptions (informed or not) about the meaning of each of those parts. As I explained in earlier chapters, nonprofit managers focus on individual programs, not whole organizations. This mental model may have been sufficient in a less complex world, but given the current challenges to non-profits, this way of thinking will not work anymore. For learning, we need integration of the parts, not separation.

Too often, managers act as if an impenetrable wall has been built between their functions and everyone else in the organization. Development officers make a decision about fundraising without discussing this with the marketing and public relations staff. Board members make a decision about changing a current program without discussing this with the staff who manage the program. Outreach staff start a new program in the community without discussing it with community partners. These functional silos in nonprofits become barriers to using the collective wisdom of staff and volunteers.

The organization must share knowledge, talent, and resources as if the barriers between units are permeable. Some examples of permeable boundaries are volunteers and staff from different units who create a shared vision and mission together, a project team that includes someone from each of the functional areas of the organization, a database of program activities that is updated and accessible by everyone in the organization, and after-action learning sessions that include all staff and volunteers. In each of these examples, communication has breached the usual barriers among staff functional areas and between staff and volunteers.

Learning to Take Risks

Organizations do not learn when they do the same things in the same way over and over again. They must take risks in order to learn. They learn from their successes, but also they learn from mistakes that are the consequence of trying something new. Speaking about change in the Massachusetts Department of Social Services (a government agency that partners with many community-based nonprofits), Harry Spence said,

> To realize continuous improvement, we have to be able to identify, safely acknowledge, and learn from error as quickly as possible, and then build systems to insulate against the damaging consequences of inevitable mistakes while reducing the frequency of those mistakes. We cannot accomplish this by constantly punishing ordinary human error. Certainly, there need to be consequences for negligence or dereliction of duty, but if I were held to an error-free standard, I wouldn't survive a single day of work here, nor would anyone else. (Saposnick, 2003, p. 10)

Discouragement of risk taking is often subtle and outside of awareness of leaders. When a nonprofit CEO frequently asks staff for reports on the number of clients served and year-to-date expenses, what is the message? By not asking about outcomes for clients or the quality of service or new connections in the community or what has been learned about providing services, the message is clear: "We value activity, not risk taking." Staff will focus their efforts on increasing client load and decreasing costs, not on creativity and innovation.

Risk taking is only a problem when managers don't learn from the successes and failures. They often have a mixed message in their heads about mistakes (i.e., failures). They have a troublesome dichotomy in their thinking: (a) We learn from our mistakes (i.e., mistakes are a good thing), and (b) only success should be rewarded (i.e., mistakes are a bad thing) (Tugend, 2007). Although managers know, intellectually, that "everyone makes mistakes" and mistakes are just part of risk taking and being creative, managers fear failure and being exposed as less than perfect. Schoemaker and Gunther (2006), in an article titled "The Wisdom of Deliberate Mistakes," say that managers invest much time and energy on trying to avoid mistakes. They argue that, instead, managers should take some actions that are likely to fail in order to provide themselves with the opportunity for learning.

Social entrepreneurs do not have the same fear of mistakes as others seem to have. In a story in the December 2007 issue of *Inc. Magazine* titled "Everybody Wants to Save the World," the author, Dalia Fahmy, tells the story of serial entrepreneur Troy Wiseman, who started a philanthropic drive in 1992 to establish orphanages around the world and discovered after 12 years and investing hundreds of thousands of dollars of his own money that many of the orphanages didn't exist or weren't using his money wisely, and there was no impact. At that point, he changed everything about his philanthropy in order to achieve greater accountability and success. Wiseman said, "Entrepreneurs aren't scared of making mistakes. We make our mistakes. And we learn from them."

Organizations that want new solutions to old problems, want creativity and innovation in their operations and products, and want employees to "think outside the box" and to "walk the talk" need to allow managers to make mistakes and learn from those experiences. I would argue that this learning cannot be left to chance. At a minimum, all mistakes (errors, failures, screw-ups, etc.) should be followed by a nonpunitive conversation between manager and supervisor about what happened, what was learned, and what should be done now to be successful in the future.

Learning to Connect People

Much of the most critical learning we do in organizations cannot be done alone. Learning how to lead others, do strategic planning, manage projects, and manage finances all require interaction with others. This kind of learning depends on the psychological safety and support of others. We learn from and through each other. Therefore, nonprofits need to find ways to connect people and create learning communities within their organizations.

Groups of staff act like a learning community when there is a feeling of connectedness among the members; when everyone considers himself or herself to be a member of that community; when there is continuity between generations (eventually, new members add to or replace the knowledge of old members); and when there is a common purpose and shared aspirations. Wenger (n.d.) calls this connectedness a "community of practice." He defines it as "people who share a concern or a passion for something they do and learn how to do it better as they interact regularly." According to Wenger, these groups have a "shared domain of interest" and a shared competence in that domain. They engage in discussion and activities together and provide mutual support, although they often work alone. They are practitioners who, over time, share their tools and methods with each other.

Examples of these communities are managers who meet monthly to discuss new and classic books related to organizational behavior; administrative staff who participate in a listserv on procedures, best practices, and advice giving; and human services workers who come together quarterly to examine their workplace processes and systems to ensure that they are maximizing benefits for clients. And then there are the ubiquitous noontime, brown-bag lunches that are arranged whenever staff or volunteers have a topic that they want to discuss with others. Each of these examples offers an opportunity for organizational learning.

Learning About Structure

The challenge for nonprofit leaders is to change an entire nonprofit into a learning community. To do this, you must attend to the structure of the organization as well as the other elements that I have already described. Is it a structure that fosters community in the sense of connectedness, membership, continuity, common purpose, and shared aspirations? A rigid hierarchy, although appealing from a control standpoint, does not promote a sense of connectedness among employees. The boxes and lines on that organizational chart say more about separation than they say about interconnectedness.

For example, a large, private foundation was organized around separate disciplines, much like a university, each with its own administrative staff (secretaries and assistants) and its own set of program officers. In typical hierarchical fashion, these grant makers reported to an executive for that program area, who reported to another executive, who reported to the president. Status, recognition, and power within the culture of the organization came from the size of the portfolio under the control of a program area and from how successful they were in paying out all of the designated funds each year. Organizational boundaries had been constructed around people, money, and information. This structure was designed for restraining behavior, and it did that quite well.

Typical of many nonprofits, this structure did not optimize learning. It discouraged shared goals, shared information, widespread cooperation, risk taking, frank evaluation, and sincere reflection. The organization's energy went into maintaining the bureaucratic structure rather than enhancing individual and group learning.

A popular saying in the systems thinking field is, "If you continue to do things the way you've been doing them, you'll continue to get the results you've been getting." You must change the structure of the organization if you want to achieve different results. So, the question for you is, "How can you get a large (or not so large), complex organization to understand how its structure, both formal and informal, operates to inhibit optimal results and then agree on changes to structure that will improve outcomes?"

Mission and strategy should determine structure, not the other way around. A structure that promotes learning is one that encourages connections across departments and disciplines and forms and unforms cross-functional teams as needed to achieve goals. This means that supervisory and reporting responsibilities are constantly in flux, responsibility and authority are dispersed throughout the organization, and lines of communication are dynamic and informal.

Evaluative Inquiry

As with individuals and teams, the process of inquiry and making meaning out of the answers facilitates learning in nonprofits, from the very large to the very small. They learn to function more effectively as a total organization when they are engaged together in seeking answers to important questions.

However, you must ask the tough questions. You must help staff understand the relationship between their actions and program outputs and outcomes, and between these results and achieving the strategic goals of the organization (Osborne & Plastrik, 2000). You must go beyond describing discrete program activities. You must look at how structure, culture, leadership, communication, knowledge management, and the physical environment affect the results you are getting. What can be learned from these effects? What does this tell you about how the organization should change?

Argyris (1977) calls this "double-loop" learning. It means challenging the beliefs and assumptions that underlie our actions and then learning from this process. Single-loop learning is what all of us do every day. We observe the consequences of something that happened in the organization, and we try to learn from that event. Let's say a management support organization offers a workshop on "Ethics in Nonprofit Management." If the attendance is high, they take that as an indication of high need and high demand. If the attendance is low, they take that as an indication of little need and little demand. This is single-loop learning. However, if they ask the question, "Is a workshop the best way to help nonprofit managers learn to behave ethically?" and then ask, "What is the best way to increase awareness of ethical issues and create more responsible nonprofits in our community?" and then use the answer to this question to develop a way of meeting this need, then they are practicing double-loop learning. They are challenging the underlying assumption that workplace ethics can be shaped by a workshop alone.

In the early 1990s, the Rheedlen Centers for Children and Families, a nonprofit in the Harlem community of New York City, had a mission of helping one child at a time stay in school with the typical social service programs, such as after-school, truancy prevention, and antiviolence training. The president of Rheedlen became frustrated with the limited impact of this approach on the thousands of children living in poverty in that community. The organization reexamined its mission and goals. They decided that they had to do something about families, schools, and the community as a whole if all children in poverty were going to succeed in education. As a result, the organization changed its direction dramatically. Now their vision is success for all children in a 60-block area of central Harlem. The organization is now called the Harlem Children's Zone, and its focus is all children who are not succeeding within that zone. This change in mission requires that the organization address problems in schools, families, and the community as a whole (Tough, 2004).

This is an example of double-loop learning. Rheedlen challenged its own assumptions and beliefs about successful children and successful communities and then changed the organization accordingly. The Rheedlen Centers could have continued to help one child at a time stay in school with a variety of after-school programs, and they could learn to be very good at that, but this approach would only put bandages on a problem that, with deeper reflection, clearly needed radical surgery.

Concerned with a growing waiting list and unsatisfactory outcomes for their graduates, Youth Villages, a residential program for youth, began examining their underlying assumptions about what was best for kids. They investigated other programs and determined that there was a better model. What they found was a program that "turned the basic residential model of care on its ear in that it was focused on the family and the home environment instead of being focused on improving the young person's behavior in a more isolated and protected environment" (McCambridge, 2006, p. 16). Then, they "convinced the state that they shouldn't be buying beds; they should buy outcomes, successful outcomes" (p. 17). The executive director of Youth Villages said,

> We essentially restarted the agency. We rewrote our values and reconstructed our practice to reflect what we learned was in the best interests of the kids—which in most cases was to stay at home with support for the whole family. (p. 17)

Using this model, Youth Villages became a successful, $80 million, multistate agency. This change can be attributed to double-loop learning and the program using new information to examine itself and decide what is the best direction for its customers.

Put up a learning mirror in front of the organization and ask staff if they like what they see. They can accept or reject the image, but they are changed in the process. They discover things about themselves of which they were previously unaware. They have beliefs confirmed or disproved. They might learn that they can look at themselves critically and nothing painful will happen. And they will learn how to learn about themselves as an organization.

Methods for Learning at the Whole Organization Level

Getting your arms around the whole organization can be a daunting task. Nonprofits of more than a handful of staff become complex entities. This complexity is likely to be overwhelming unless you use a coherent, learning-based approach to achieve understanding. Methods that lead to this whole organization learning emphasize integration of people, units, and information rather than their separation. Some of these methods are described below.

Organizational Self-Assessment

The place to begin is with organizational self-assessment. The term *self-assessment* represents a variety of tools for evaluating an organization to assist in learning and change. It often takes the form of a survey instrument that asks staff, as well as volunteers and other partners, to report on the performance of the organization. Results are compared to a set of standards or internally derived expectations.

External consultants and nonprofit managers have debated the efficacy of designing and managing this kind of assessment. One side argues the need for neutrality and objectivity, and the other side argues for relevance and control. Ideally, you should incorporate both sides of the argument. Use an internally driven assessment to build a sense of ownership of the results and to develop the competency to repeat this kind of assessment periodically. Use externally driven assessment to take advantage of the expertise and "fresh eyes" of someone who doesn't have a vested interest in seeing only positive results. However, the practicalities of time and money will have much to say about whether you can do one or both.

When designing the self-assessment, even if you are using an off-the-shelf survey instrument, involve all of the key stakeholders.

Maybe you will not be able to engage all employees and volunteers in this discussion and planning, but you can include representatives of the various employee and volunteer groups. Their input will be vital, and this process of including them will build their acceptance and facilitate organization-wide learning.

The Denison Culture Survey (Adkins & Stewart, 2004) is an example of a tool that can be used for self-assessment. This instrument measures four traits, each with three management practices:

Mission—the degree to which people understand the direction of the organization and how they can contribute to achieving those goals; this trait includes the attributes of vision, strategic direction and intent, and goals and objectives.

Involvement—the degree to which people are engaged in achieving organizational goals and objectives; this trait includes capability development, team orientation, and empowerment.

Adaptability—the ability of the organization to respond to changing needs of customers and stakeholders; this trait includes creating change, customer focus, and organizational learning.

Consistency—the degree to which core values and internal systems affect the effectiveness of the organization; this trait includes core values, agreement, and coordination and integration.

After hiring a new CEO, the Family Health Council of Central Pennsylvania (FHCCP) used the Denison Culture Survey to examine the strengths and weaknesses of its culture. FHCCP builds community-based health networks for the purpose of ensuring affordable, accessible health care for central Pennsylvania. It administered the survey in 1999 and again in 2001. Findings were reviewed by the board of directors, the leadership team, the staff, and customers. This reflective process was used to clarify the strategic direction of the organization, develop an annual plan, and connect employees to the vision and strategy. Although not without its trials and tribulations, the process resulted in the nonprofit making significant changes that contributed to improvement in all of their key performance indicators: clients served, revenue, customer satisfaction, and size of staff.

Benchmarking

Xerox Corp. is credited with being the first to use benchmarking as a strategic tool (Hequet, 1993). They found that you can learn much from the practices of other organizations and from the process of comparing your organization to other organizations. This is true whether comparing one unit to another unit in your organization or going outside to other organizations, nonprofits or for-profits, that do something well. Either of these activities is called *benchmarking*. Although not used much by smaller nonprofits, except in very informal ways, it is a useful tool for any kind of organization.

Visit other nonprofits (and for-profit businesses, for that matter) to understand their practices. However, simply visiting is not benchmarking. Being a "tourist" does not necessarily result in organizational learning. Like visiting a new city while on vacation, you will not understand the history and culture without a plan and a guide. Maybe you want to learn how others manage a donor database, or conduct their board meetings, or respond to customer problems, or work with government and business partners in the community. Whatever it is, have a plan and a set of questions you want to have answered. To ensure learning from benchmarking, take your organization through this process:

Step 1: Conduct an organizational self-assessment.

Step 2: Decide what you want to learn from benchmarking.

Step 3: Examine what is being done by other organizations in the area in which you are interested; ask your questions.

Step 4: Use that information to plan change in your own organization.

Step 5: Support that change through training and development activities.

The key to this whole process is doing an adequate self-assessment at the front end of the process that lets you know specifically what needs to be changed. This requires collecting data that give you confidence that you understand fully the depth and breadth of the problem. It is not enough to be curious. If you try to benchmark with a superficial understanding of your need, you will not know what organization to select for benchmarking, you will not know what to look for in that organization, you will not know how to apply their approach to your organization, and you will not be able to build support and acceptance from the people who have to implement the changes you are recommending.

If you do not understand the problem, you might not ask the right questions. A critical question that should be asked during the self-assessment phase is, "Should we be using this process in the first place?" This is the kind of question that can result in double-loop learning. It challenges underlying values of the decision.

Before you even embark on a benchmarking project, prepare the organization for learning and change. Employees and volunteers must accept that they are not the best in everything and that they can learn from others, especially others outside of your own organization. Prepare them to use the information that you collect; they might have to change some things, and they might have to train people to do things differently. Set the expectation that staff will need to develop knowledge, skills, and attitudes to make the necessary changes.

World Café

The World Café process was developed in the late 1990s by Juanita Brown and David Isaacs at Whole System Associates to create the conditions for having a learning conversation among all participants in a large group. Recognizing that collaborative learning is an essential aspect of a sustainable community, the World Café was created to help an entire community collaborate for the purpose of learning. The World Café creates a network of conversations around questions that lead the group to a shared understanding. It is a way of sharing knowledge and accessing the collective intelligence of the community, regardless of how that community is defined.

Almost any number of participants can engage in this activity. The only restrictions on number of participants are the size of the space you have in which to meet, the number of people available to assist in facilitating the event, and your capacity for collecting and summarizing the information that is collected during the event.

Through a conversation that is based on the principles and processes of dialogue (see Chapter 5), participants listen to each other, surface underlying assumptions and beliefs, and achieve greater shared understanding without the pressure for solutions. Agreement is not important. Listening to all ideas and opinions is important. You should be concerned about clarity of meaning, not the facts. Begin the conversation with an important, galvanizing question. This is the one question that, if answered, would make the most difference to the total group.

The World Café is characterized by the following:

Hospitable Space—a space for conversation in small groups that is informal, inviting, and safe for everyone (usually similar to café-style seating with small tables and four to six chairs around each table)

Questions That Matter—a focus on a question that is powerful enough to motivate participants to seek collective insight

Spirit of Discovery—conversations that are more like dialogue than normal, everyday discussion; participants give information and ask questions without trying to convince someone else to take a particular position on an issue

Shared Listening—participants listen for connections and themes that run through the conversation; these connections and themes are written or drawn on paper at the center of each table and left behind as participants change tables several times; a host stays at the table to provide continuity to the next group that comes to the table

Awareness of Connections—connections are made among the conversations that occur at each table for each table group and then among all of the tables (Brown, 2001).

An example is an event that emphasized the "world" in "World Café." This was a meeting at the Salzburg Seminar in Salzburg, Austria. Seventy leaders of nongovernmental (nonprofit) organizations from around the world, trying to build democracy and civil society in their own countries, met for a weeklong session of study of the independent sector. The setting was the ballroom of a spectacular castle, the Schloss Leopoldskron, built in the 1700s and restored in the 1920s. It is a very special meeting place with a long tradition of serious discussions about democracy in war-torn and developing nations.

The goals of using the World Café at the Salzburg Seminar were to

- build participation and involvement
- establish shared ownership for learning
- begin to share underlying beliefs and values
- set the tone and process for the rest of the week
- connect every participant to every other participant

All of the participants gathered in the Great Hall of the Schloss. The purposes and procedure for a World Café were explained to them. It was stressed that the World Café is a place for involvement, sharing, networking, and connections. It is a place for thoughtful conversation about a significant question. It is about dialogue, which involves careful listening to each other, not arguing for a position. Questions are used to explore ideas and weave connections among ideas. This means that everyone should listen for themes that flow through the comments, observations, and questions. It is not about looking for answers. Participants were encouraged to talk from their own experience. It was emphasized that this activity just starts the conversation that would continue throughout the remainder of the week.

Then, the procedures for this World Café were explained to the group. These procedures were as follows:

1. Participants take a seat at any of the eight café tables around the room.

2. Each person introduces himself or herself briefly to the other people at the table.

3. One person volunteers to be a scribe and to write notes on flipchart paper that covers each table.

4. Participants talk about their responses to a question, which, for this Café, was "From your practical experience, what have you learned from the past 10 years about the independent sector, and what are the unresolved issues and dilemmas?"

5. The conversation lasts about 20 minutes, and at the end of the 20 minutes, one person volunteers to stay at the table and everyone else scatters to other tables.

6. The person who stays at the table gives a brief report on highlights of the previous conversation to the new people at that table.

7. Each new table group continues the conversation.

This process was repeated twice more so that everyone participated in a total of three different small group conversations.

At the beginning, participants were given a brief demonstration of the process. The methods of conversation (through dialogue) and note taking (on flipchart paper draped across each table) were explained and demonstrated. After the three rounds of conversations ended, one person from each table was invited to call out a theme that cut across the three conversations at their tables. That generated a list of key issues and questions that helped direct the discussion for the week of learning together.

Appreciative Inquiry

The basic idea behind Appreciative Inquiry, as originally proposed by David Cooperrider (Cooperrider, Sorensen, Whitney, & Yaeger, 2000), is to bring to everyone's awareness the positive experiences and successes of the organization. Rather than analyzing problems and trying to identify what is wrong with the organization, which is the most common approach, the focus of Appreciative Inquiry is on what is right and how we can learn from and build on these strengths.

A three-step process has been proposed for preparing to conduct Appreciative Inquiry in a large-group meeting (Zemke, 1999):

Step 1: Choose the topic and put it in positive terms.

Step 2: Create questions that will stimulate participants to report positive examples.

Step 3: Ask the questions of everyone who is a source of the information; keep in mind that asking questions is an intervention into the life of the organization, so err on the side of inclusion and listen carefully to the answers.

Once these preparatory steps have been completed, you can begin the phases of what is called the 4-D process (Zemke, 1999):

Discovery: Report the stories from the preparatory steps and discuss their significance for the future of the organization.

Dreaming: Discuss what everyone wants the organization to look like in 5 years; come to consensus on a vision, mission, and strategic goals.

Design: Using the vision for the future, decide on a set of driving concepts and principles by which the organization will operate.

Destiny: Support application and sustaining what was decided in the first three phases.

Four statements guide this strategy:

1. Appreciate *What Is.*

2. Imagine *What Might Be.*

3. Determine *What Should Be.*

4. Create *What Will Be.*

Appreciative Inquiry was used to evaluate the African Women's Media Center (AWMC), located in Senegal, West Africa. The purpose of the AWMC is to help African women journalists be successful, especially in addressing issues important to women in Africa (Catsambas & Webb, 2003). The evaluation of AWMC at that time was intended to take stock of the organization, inform their strategic planning process, and help them continue to improve.

Using the Appreciative Inquiry questions adapted for the situation, external evaluators conducted interviews with staff, current and prospective advisory group members, and a wide array of other stakeholders from across Africa. From this process, the AWMC clarified its role, received feedback about its programs, identified networking in Africa as a major priority, examined its sustainability, and assessed its leadership needs. In the process, staff learned a different way of working together. Evaluators observed that "staff members are asking questions differently than they did in the past, now with a deliberate focus on how to improve, grow, and learn from their successes" (Catsambas & Webb, 2003, p. 48).

Large-Scale Learning Events

What if you could get your whole organization, or a large part of it, together in one location to experience self-discovery, teamwork, problem solving, and the creation of a shared vision of the future? Wouldn't this be a great opportunity for learning? This is the purpose of a number of event-driven, large-group methods. What these various methods have in common is a large number of staff representing all parts of the organization; engaging in a time-limited event; and participating in new ways that challenge the bureaucratic, hierarchical, command-and-control cultures that are typical of the participants' organizations.

For several of these designs, as with World Café, the only factors that limit the number of participants is the size of the room, the logistics of bringing that many people together at the same time, and the number and capability of the facilitators. For example, the "Whole-Scale Change" design was used for 2,000 employees of one very large organization. The cavernous rooms of a downtown convention center had to be rented for this 3-day process that included whole group and small group activities.

Some of the other large-scale designs that have proved very effective and the people who have developed them are as follows:

- Future Search—Marvin Weisbord (1987)
- Preferred Futuring—Ronald Lippitt and Lawrence L. Lippitt (Lippitt, 1998)
- Whole-Scale Change—Kathleen Dannemiller (Dannemiller, James, & Tolchinsky, 1999)
- Open Space Technology—Harrison Owen (1997)
- The Conference Model—Emily M. Axelrod and Richard H. Axelrod (1999)

Each of these resources offers a framework and tools for whole organization change.

An event that combined several of these methods was a day-long meeting of the staff and board members of two social service nonprofits that had recently merged their organizations. The purpose of the meeting was to build a shared vision for the newly merged agency and initiate an overall strategic planning process. The meeting mixed the nearly 300 employees and board members from the two organizations into eight-person groups around small tables in a large meeting hall. After presentations by a few of the staff on the history of the two organizations, each of the table groups was asked to brainstorm a list of what they were proud of in the new organization and what they were sorry about in terms of how the new organization is functioning. Then, the groups listed the values and beliefs that underlie what they do as an organization. These values and beliefs were called out to the whole group, and a master list was created at the front of the room.

An environmental scan came next. The groups listed the trends and events locally, statewide, and nationally that would affect their work in the future. Again, these were called out from each group and a master list was created. Finally, the groups, taking into consideration what they knew about the past, present, and future, developed scenarios of their vision for the future of the agency. These scenarios were posted on walls around the room, and participants were asked to read them and vote for their preferences. The event ended with a charge to agency leaders to form task groups to work on more specific goals and action plans for achieving each of the goals that had been identified. This large-scale learning event not only identified goals for the newly merged agency, it also helped the staff learn how to do this kind of visioning and strategic planning process.

Summary

Like individuals and teams, organizations can learn, and they can learn how to learn. They do this by creating a culture of learning. They create structures and processes that are designed to support learning. They facilitate sharing of information, knowledge, and practices among employees and volunteers. They create a safe environment in which staff feel like they can take risks and not worry about being punished for doing so. Organizational silos that separate people and functions are eliminated, or at least minimized. Meetings and large-scale events are designed to break down these silos, encourage risk taking, and improve communication. This chapter describes methods that can be used to help organizations create this kind of culture.

7

Community Learning

*I don't divide the world into the weak and the strong, or
the successes and the failures. . . . I divide the world into
the learners and nonlearners.*

—Benjamin Barber

Nonprofits have an obligation to serve their communities. The
definition of a nonprofit's community is broad. It could be
geographic, as in the case of a homeless shelter (e.g., Detroit Coalition
on Temporary Shelters) or a museum (e.g., Minneapolis Institute of
Arts). It could be membership based, as in the case of a professional
association (e.g., American Medical Association) or a national youth
service organization (e.g., Girl Scouts of America). It could be constituency based, as in the case of environmental advocacy (e.g., Sierra
Club) and issue-focused organizations (e.g., Brady Campaign to Prevent
Gun Violence). Regardless of the kind of community, a nonprofit can
help create a culture of learning that will assist both the nonprofit and
that community in achieving their goals. This chapter explores ways in
which nonprofits can contribute to community learning.

Your nonprofit does not exist in isolation. It is an interdependent
part of a larger system of individuals, government agencies, businesses,
philanthropies, and other nonprofits that are influenced by economics,
politics, social issues, and the environment. Your organization's

capacity to meet the needs of customers is tied directly to the capacity of this larger community system. For example, a welfare-to-work program might be providing exceptional training and counseling to unemployed mothers. However, if jobs are not available in the community, all the training and counseling in the world will not make a long-term difference for those women. A community orchestra might be successful in producing great music and attracting top-notch soloists. But if patrons believe that it is not safe to attend these productions because of the location of the hall or insufficient security, then talented musicians and a superb conductor will do little to increase attendance. A hospice agency might provide exceptional care to dying patients, but unless this agency attracts strong board members from the local community and receives donations that cover the difference in cost between what patients pay and the true cost of services, that agency will not be able to survive.

Nonprofits cannot function in isolation. To succeed, they must nurture and sustain interdependence with other nonprofits, government agencies, and the private sector. The problems of our society are too great and the needs too complex to go it alone. They need strong partners and strong communities.

Grant and Crutchfield (2007) studied 12 highly successful nonprofits and concluded that community interdependence is a key to effectiveness:

> High-impact nonprofits work with and through organizations and individuals outside themselves to create more impact than they ever could have achieved alone. They build social movements and fields; they transform business, government, other nonprofits, and individuals; and they change the world around them.

The authors identified six practices of high-impact nonprofits, one of which has to do with adaptability, which they define as "mastered the ability to listen, learn, and modify their approach on the basis of external cues." In other words, these nonprofits are continually learning and learning how to learn from their interactions with partners in the wider community.

This dependence on partners is exacerbated by the trend toward flatter, leaner organizations. With the intent of cutting costs while also making large organizations less bureaucratic and more nimble in their response to new situations and new opportunities, levels of administration have been eliminated. This should increase communication within and among departments. However, with fewer layers of administration and fewer administrators and staff trying to accomplish the same goals, there is a greater need to create partnerships with other organizations in the community that can support the mission.

Nonprofits have a special role to play in building capacity of a community. As stated in a report sponsored by the National Civic League (2001):

> Nonprofits must take the lead. Businesses are inherently competitive, and government agencies are inherently insular. Both of those traits are at odds with effective collaboration. Thus, it falls to nonprofits to be the catalyst. (p. 11)

Of course, there are business and government exceptions. That is, some business leaders do invest in community change, and some legislators and bureaucrats will participate in government transformation. However, nonprofits can get the ball rolling. It is within their missions to assess community-wide needs, evaluate progress toward meeting those needs, and provide feedback that stimulates all sectors to respond.

The Minneapolis Foundation took the lead on a student achievement and scholarship program in the Twin Cities. Destination 2010 is a collaborative effort of Minneapolis and St. Paul public schools; local organizations (summer camps, Big Brothers Big Sisters, and others); government agencies; and volunteers. The primary goal of the program is school retention and college enrollment for a cohort of students scheduled to graduate in 2010. A secondary goal is transformation of the educational system so that all kids can succeed. From their initial experiences with the program, The Minneapolis Foundation learned that keeping kids in school and making progress would require broad community support and effort.

In Minneapolis and St. Paul, the nonprofit, government, and business sectors are learning how to work together to improve the lives of children, transform schools, and enhance the quality of life. This is what is needed to solve the most intractable problems in our communities. Nonprofits can and should take the lead, but it will continue to be a collaborative learning effort for all sectors.

Community Feedback and Reflection

Learning in communities, as with individuals, teams, and whole organizations, is achieved through feedback and reflection. This is challenging given the complexity of communities. Geographic communities, in particular, tend to lack the shared focus that is necessary for learning. However, this focus can be achieved over time by carefully and strategically orchestrating cooperation among the various segments.

Communities need credible, consensus-building, visible leadership that can convene all sectors. People from different social and economic strata of a community will have widely divergent interests. Bringing these individuals and groups together requires the convening power of strong leaders who are perceived to be fair and neutral by the general community.

Another important aspect of working with communities is to focus on assets as well as needs. The asset-based approach starts by taking an inventory of individual, group, institution, and community-wide resources. Then, these resources are used to strengthen the educational, economic, cultural, and social quality of life of that community. The community starts with what it has, not what it lacks.

Traditionally, policymakers and professional service providers focus on the deficiencies and problems of a neighborhood, town, or city. They look at what is missing in terms of indicators such as low-performing schools, crime, homelessness, poverty, substance abuse, violence, disease, pollution, urban sprawl, and underutilized land. This approach does not convey the true nature of a community. Residents see themselves as victims, dependent on nonprofit services and expertise from outside their communities. Efforts become fragmented as resources shift from one problem and one person to the next. Money is used to put bandages on short-term solutions rather than investing in the long-term health of the community.

With an asset-based approach, the emphasis is on strengths, not deficiencies. It is focused on local leadership and local capabilities, self-reliance and long-term sustainability, relationships and social capital, and interdependence and interconnectedness. These are the elements of a strong community, one that knows how to solve its own problems and maximize the quality of life for residents.

Kretzmann and McKnight (1993) offer five steps to "asset-based community development":

1. Mapping completely the capacities and assets of individuals, citizens' associations and local institutions. [See their Community Assets Map and Capacity Inventory, pp. 19–25]

2. Building relationships among local assets for mutually beneficial problem-solving within the community.

3. Mobilizing the community's assets fully for economic development and information sharing purposes.

4. Convening as broadly representative a group as possible for the purposes of building a community vision and plan.

5. Leveraging activities, investments and resources from outside the community to support asset-based, locally-defined development. (p. 345)

This is an approach that is "asset-based, internally focused and relationship driven" (Kretzmann & McKnight, 1993, p. 10). The process is one of determining the available resources in the community that people and institutions can apply to solving local problems. The solutions are usually about connections. That is, connecting individuals, groups, and institutions so that they can combine their knowledge, skills, tools, physical resources, and financial resources.

Different approaches to building successful communities have these generic steps in common:

Step 1: Identify the needs and assets of the community.

Step 2: Involve all segments of the community.

Step 3: Connect various segments of the community and build relationships.

Step 4: Share information among stakeholders.

Step 5: Keep stakeholders informed.

Step 6: Assess progress and make adjustments.

Step 7: Evaluate outcomes, intended and unintended.

Although not always successful because of the complexity of this kind of change, good examples exist. Many communities, from neighborhoods to cities to multicounty regions to entire states to nations, have engaged in learning and capacity building. None of the efforts in these communities has been a permanent fix. Each has required constant building and rebuilding as local people, conditions, and needs change over time. Kansas City, Missouri; Chattanooga, Tennessee; the state of Oregon; and the nation of Sweden are examples of communities that have worked on learning how to build and maintain success over time.

Kansas City

The Alliance for National Renewal (ANR), an initiative of the National Civic League (2001), undertook a project to examine examples of community-based change. By capturing the lessons from various community improvement efforts, ANR hoped to assist those efforts and other communities in their quest for change and an enhanced quality of life.

The Kansas City Neighborhood Alliance (KCNA) was one of the community capacity-building efforts that ANR evaluated. KCNA was established in 1979 "to build the capacity of Kansas City's neighborhoods to become safe, strong, stable and attractive places where people are proud to live" (National Civic League, 2001, p. 19). This community capacity building was prompted by a concern about declining single-family home ownership, in particular for lower-income residents. KCNA addressed this problem by buying and rehabilitating homes and by making loans available to previously excluded families. In addition, KCNA offered leadership training and mentoring for neighborhood leaders. This effort built capacity by teaching these leaders how to participate and lead a community problem-solving process that results in important outcomes, a process that these leaders could continue to use with their communities.

ANR identified valuable lessons from the community capacity-building effort in Kansas City and elsewhere:

1. Successful collaborative efforts can be initiated by any sector of the community, but to be successful these efforts must eventually involve all sectors.

2. The best collaborations are those that grow out of outcomes orientations, but also are those that pay attention to the processes through which those outcomes are to be achieved.

3. A shared vision helps overcome sector differences, organizational turf issues, bridges demographic diversity and unites distinct jurisdictions.

4. There is a need for organizations to facilitate collaborative efforts.

5. The ability of a community to address its challenges is in large part dependent upon the quality of its civic infrastructure.

6. Collaboration can take many forms and serve multiple purposes, but regardless of the form or purpose can add value to community building efforts. (National Civic League, 2001, pp. 41–47)

ANR learned the critical importance of collaboration. In order to make truly significant change in a community, you have to find ways for all sectors to collaborate. The nature of this collaboration in a particular community is shaped by the civic infrastructure, which is the sum of skills, processes, and relationships that allow communities to come together and solve problems. Using these methods of collaboration and adapting these methods to the civic infrastructure of a community are skills that can and should be taught to community leaders.

Chattanooga

Another city that has made tremendous progress in quality of life because of its community learning and capacity-building efforts is Chattanooga, Tennessee. In 1969, Chattanooga was ranked the most polluted city in the United States. Since then, through the ongoing collaboration of citizen groups, local government officials, the Chamber of Commerce, private ventures, and nonprofit organizations, the city has become a model of sustainable environment (Rogge, 1998).

A nonprofit organization was formed to revitalize the city. By conducting a community-wide survey of needs, holding public forums, keeping up an ongoing community visioning process, identifying and refining a broad set of goals and projects, and forming citizen groups to address those goals and projects, Chattanooga was able to make dramatic progress. These efforts resulted in a "network of sustainable community development initiatives" (Rogge, 1998, p. 110). The initiatives evolved into pollution control programs, conservation projects, institutions that celebrate the ecological diversity of the region, and riverfront development to bring people back to recreational and residential use of the river.

These separate initiatives and accomplishments are not community capacity building in themselves. It is the ongoing process that Chattanooga has put in place for identifying needs and continually evaluating progress that makes it an effective and sustainable community. The city has learned how to learn from its citizens, businesses, and government agencies.

Oregon

An example of state-wide community learning and capacity building through evaluation is the state of Oregon. This state has used a results-driven measurement system since 1989. This system is based on a set of strategic goals and measurable benchmarks that is revised by citizen committees, policymakers, and experts every 2 years. The emphasis is on results, not activities, and on progress, not a score.

The change in Oregon began with support from a courageous governor who received a variance from federal requirements in how Oregon used block grant money. Citizen groups were convened throughout the state to develop consensus around capacity-building goals and to identify specific, measurable indicators of progress toward those goals. For example, anti-abortion groups and pro-choice groups could not agree on tactics, but they could agree that unwanted teenage pregnancy was not a good thing; therefore, their shared goal was to decrease the number of unwanted teenage pregnancies.

These kinds of discussions led to the creation of benchmarks that focused the attention of Oregon communities. Baseline measures were recorded and the benchmarks were tracked over time. Oregon, under the title "Oregon Shines," used the benchmarks to assess its progress toward the achievement of broad strategic goals as indicators of social, economic, and environmental well-being.

For the year 2003, the goals were as follows:

1. Quality jobs for all Oregonians

2. Engaged, caring and safe communities

3. Healthy, sustainable surroundings. (Oregon Progress Board, 2003)

Oregon Shines prepared a chart of these goals and the more specific objectives that represented progress toward these goals (see Table 7.1). Within these objectives are "benchmarks." Benchmarks are measurable indicators; they indicate that the objectives are being achieved. Examples of some of these benchmarks are the following:

Net job growth: a. urban counties, b. rural counties

Explanation: This measures change in average employment between the listed year and the year prior. The benchmark is stratified by urban and rural counties. Urban counties include: Benton, Clackamas, Columbia, Deschutes, Jackson, Lane, Linn, Marion, Multnomah, Polk, Washington, and Yamhill. Target: Target set by Oregon Progress Board. Data source: Covered employment and payrolls, Oregon Employment Department.

Pregnancy rate per 1,000 females: a. ages 10–14, b. ages 15–17

Explanation: The sum of resident live births and induced abortions among females ages 10–17 divided by the estimated population of females ages 10–17. The rate does not include spontaneous abortions and fetal deaths. The pregnancy rate includes live births to Oregon residents and abortions for Oregon residents regardless of where the abortion was performed. Out-of-state abortions for Oregon residents may be underreported because some states where Oregon residents go to have abortions do not report the patient's state of residence. Target: Target set by the Health Services Cluster. Targets are aggressive but realistic because there are many programs, including a Governor's Task Force, related to preventing teen pregnancy. Data sources: Oregon Department of Human Services, Health Services Cluster, Center for Health Statistics, Oregon Vital Statistics Annual Report. Population estimates for Oregon published annually by the Center for Population Research and Census, School of Urban and Public Affairs, Portland State University.

Table 7.1   Oregon Shines II Framework

Oregon's Strategic Vision: "A prosperous Oregon that excels in all spheres of life."		
Goal 1 Quality Jobs for All Oregonians	*Goal 2 Safe, Caring and Engaged Communities*	*Goal 3 Healthy, Sustainable Surroundings*
Objectives	*Objectives*	*Objectives*
1. Oregon will have a world-class workforce—well educated, skilled and working—to keep Oregon's economy competitive in the global marketplace.	1. All aspects of society will encourage responsible parenting and adult mentoring of children.	1. Oregon will support thoughtful growth management strategies.
2. Oregon will be one of the top 10 states in America to start and grow a technology generating company.	2. Oregon will be the leader in developing state and local partnerships that address the root causes of social problems.	2. Oregon will have a progressive system for resolving natural resource management issues.
3. State agencies should coordinate their efforts with local communities to diversify and strengthen the economies of rural Oregon.	3. Oregon will prevent crime by emphasizing cost-effective prevention programs that avoid future incarceration costs.	3. Oregon state government will support rural communities in solving natural resource dilemmas at the local level.
4. More Oregon companies will export higher-valued products.	4. Oregon will be a leader in reducing personal abuse and protecting vulnerable individuals.	

Goal 1 Quality Jobs for All Oregonians	Goal 2 Safe, Caring and Engaged Communities	Goal 3 Healthy, Sustainable Surroundings
Objectives	Objectives	Objectives
5. Oregon will be a net exporter of high-end professional services by 2010.	5. More Oregonians will be healthy and self-sufficient.	
6. Oregon's policies will support small business by providing adequate infrastructure while holding down the costs of doing business.	6. More Oregonians will actively participate in strengthening their communities.	
7. Oregon's per capita income will reach the national average by 2010.		

SOURCE: Oregon Progress Board. (2003). *Is Oregon making progress? The 2003 benchmark performance report.* http://www.oregon.gov/DAS/OPB/docs/2003report/Report/2003BPR.pdf

Percent of time that the air is healthy to breathe for all Oregonians

Explanation: This benchmark measures the percent of time that air in Oregon meets the criteria for healthy air. The data are based on monitoring of Oregon air sheds for carbon monoxide, ozone, fine particulates, and other pollutants. New air quality standards and monitoring data in the future will likely require adjustment of the benchmark data. Target: Target set by Oregon Progress Board. Data source: Oregon Department of Environmental Quality, Air Quality Division.

This level of specificity is very important. It gives clarity to the intended outcome and causes everyone, from all sectors of the state-wide community, to be focused on the same thing. This increases the likelihood of success and enhances communication to citizens about what is being achieved. The intended outcomes are the same for everyone; the methods for getting to those outcomes are the prerogative of each organization in the community. And Oregon citizens have learned how to bring about meaningful change.

Oregon's benchmarks have evolved since 1989. A new Progress Board is leading Oregon Shines III, which, in 2007, reassessed progress and identified areas for change to achieve greater success. This new process, according to the Progress Board, is intended to "embrace a multi-faceted approach that will build our capacity to think more systemically, act more collaboratively, produce sustainable results and measurably transform Oregon's future" (Oregon Progress Board, 2007).

Sweden

Even an entire country can learn and build capacity for significant change through feedback and reflection. Sweden had more than 70 municipalities and 60 corporations working on sustainability under the direction of a nongovernmental organization called The Natural Step. A leading Swedish oncologist, Karl-Henrik Robèrt, recognized a link between the health of children and the natural environment. He started The Natural Step to prevent further destruction of the environment and work toward a sustainable society (Robèrt, 1997).

Similar to the Oregon Benchmarks, Robèrt and his colleagues developed consensus around a set of principles rather than prescribing solutions. Then, they encouraged various groups to examine their actions within the framework of those principles. The four principles were as follows:

1. In a sustainable society, nature is not subject to systematically increasing concentrations of substances extracted from the earth's crust.

2. In a sustainable society, nature is not subject to systematically increasing concentrations of substances produced by society.

3. In a sustainable society, nature is not subject to systematically increasing degradation by physical means.

4. In a sustainable society, human needs are met worldwide.

The Natural Step asked every company, organization, individual, family, and government agency to examine its behavior and the consequences of that behavior in light of these principles. This approach provided a way in which communities could learn about their role in creating a sustainable and healthy environment.

Ask yourself and your organization these "Natural Step" questions:

- How can we eliminate our contribution to systematic increases in concentrations of substances from the Earth's crust?
- How can we eliminate our contribution to systematic increases in concentrations of substances produced by society?
- How can we eliminate our contribution to systematic physical degradation of nature through overharvesting, depletion, foreign introductions, and other forms of modification?
- How can we contribute as much as we can to the goal of meeting human needs in our society and worldwide, going over and above all the substitution and dematerialization measures taken in meeting the first three objectives?

In each of the city, state, and nation communities described above, many people from different sectors learned how to solve problems together. They learned what questions to ask. They learned who to ask. They learned in what format to ask these questions. They learned how to use the information to plan change. They learned how to connect people from across their communities and how to collaborate. All of these learnings built the long-term capacity of these communities to continuously address their needs and solve problems. The process can be tedious and painful at times, but the rewards are great.

Methods for Learning at the Community Level

Several tools have been developed for this purpose. One is the National Civic League's Civic Index (National Civic League, 1999). This index is based on standards for a strong community.

Each community may use these categories as a starting point but then develops its own indicators. For example, the Yampa Valley Partners Community Indicators Project in Colorado used the following outline of indicator categories:

1. Our Desired Future (community vision)

2. Community Governance
   - General
   - Citizens
   - Local Government
   - Nonprofits
   - Business

3. Working Together
   - Bridging Diversity
   - Sharing Information
   - Crossing Jurisdictional Lines

4. Strengthening Our Community
   - Citizen Education
   - Community Leadership
   - Learning From Our Experiences

The importance of using civic indicators is not in having scores. The value is in engaging the community in deciding what indicators are important and in using these measures to plan, set priorities, monitor progress, make adjustments as needed, and give citizens a sense of accomplishment and pride when there is progress.

Oregon used town hall-type meetings to identify its benchmarks. Similar gatherings of community leaders and representatives of various stakeholder groups have been used in many communities across the United States to evaluate and set goals for their communities. What they have in common is giving people from all sectors of a community a structured way of examining assets and needs and then finding consensus on a set of goals. Over the course of a day or several days, groups are led through a process of brainstorming, prioritizing, and goal setting. These goals provide the direction for task groups to continue the hard work of community-wide change.

Another set of tools falls under the category of social capital assessment. Social capital is defined as the "norms and networks that enable people to work collectively to resolve problems and achieve common goals" (Healy & Hampshire, 2002, p. 228). Along with economic capital, physical capital, human capital, and cultural capital, social capital contributes to the capacity of a community.

Social capital is created by the connections that individuals and groups make with each other to achieve some benefit for themselves and others.

Under the leadership of the Saguaro Seminar on Civic Engagement in America at the John F. Kennedy School of Government at Harvard University, and with the support and participation of community foundations and other funders, the Social Capital Community Benchmark Survey was developed (Saguaro Seminar, 2001). This survey instrument asks residents questions such as the following:

1. How many of your neighbors' first names do you know?

2. How often do you attend parades or festivals?

3. Do you volunteer at your kids' school? Or help out senior citizens?

4. Do you trust your local police?

5. Do you know who your U.S. senators are?

6. Do you attend religious services? Or go to the theater?

7. Do you sign petitions? Or attend neighborhood meetings?

8. Do you think the people running your community care about you?

9. Can you make a difference?

10. How often do you visit with friends or family?

Conducting this survey can help communities bring attention to the importance of civic engagement, take stock of what they need to do to increase social capital, and monitor change in social capital over time. You might use this set of questions in your own community.

Community Capacity Assessment

The Community Capacity Assessment (see Tool 7.1) can be used to assess your local community's capacity to support the mission of your nonprofit. Given the interdependence of your nonprofit with the other institutions in the community, this tool provides a structure and focus for examining the assets that need to be maintained and the

Tool 7.1	Community Capacity Assessment				
Statement	Strongly Agree	Agree	Neutral	Disagree	Strongly Disagree
1. My nonprofit is clear about how its mission is dependent on leadership in the local community.					
2. My nonprofit is clear about how its mission is dependent on institutions in the local community.					
3. My nonprofit is clear about how its mission is dependent on resources in the local community.					
4. This community has the infrastructure needed to help my nonprofit achieve its goals.					
5. This community has the assets needed to help my nonprofit achieve its goals.					
6. This community has the local economy (including jobs) to support my nonprofit in achieving its goals.					
7. This community has the necessary quality in its educational institutions to support my nonprofit in achieving its goals.					
8. This community has the necessary quality in its cultural institutions to support my nonprofit in achieving its goals.					

Statement	Strongly Agree	Agree	Neutral	Disagree	Strongly Disagree
9. This community has the social service agencies that are needed to support my nonprofit in achieving its goals.					
10. This community has the recreational facilities that are needed to support my nonprofit in achieving its goals.					
11. This community has the public safety services that are needed to support my nonprofit in achieving its goals.					
12. This community has the health care resources needed to support my nonprofit in achieving its goals.					
13. This community has collaborative efforts among sectors to solve problems.					
14. This community has opportunities for collective learning.					
15. This community has opportunities for capacity building.					

gaps that need to be filled. It can provide an opportunity for collective learning about your community. The questions provide the basis for community self-evaluation and reflection.

Convene your staff and other stakeholders in the community to discuss these questions. Try to develop consensus around the answers. Then, use this information to discuss implications and solutions.

Summary

Communities are the fourth level of learning for nonprofits. This level builds on individual, team, and whole organization learning. Nonprofits have a dynamic interdependence with their wider communities. Nonprofits exist to serve these communities, and the success of a nonprofit is dependent on the assets and capabilities of their communities. Whether defined by geography, membership, or constituency, communities become successful through continual learning. They can learn how to assess their needs and assets, and they can learn how to use that information to continuously improve the quality of life for stakeholders. Nonprofits are in the best position to be the leaders of these learning efforts. They can convene people from government, private, and independent sectors and facilitate their collective learning. In this process, they teach communities how to achieve their goals.

8

Learning From Evaluation

It's not what you don't know that'll hurt you, it's what you do know that ain't so.

—Appalachian Mountain Proverb

The previous chapters of this book have described methods and tools for facilitating organizational learning through ongoing feedback and reflection. The purpose of those methods and tools is to raise questions and stimulate conversation about process and results. Those methods and tools are practical but often lack the precision and credibility of more formal evaluation methods and tools. In certain situations, you and other stakeholders may want to have greater confidence that evidence of progress and outcomes will "stand up in court," figuratively and sometimes literally. This is where the discipline of evaluation comes in.

Outcome-Focused Evaluation

Nonprofits need a disciplined approach to organizational learning. They need an approach that gives them confidence that they "know-what," "know-how," and "know-why." Simply asking yourself questions is a good start, but not sufficient. You must ensure that you have accurate, reliable, and useful data, and that these data are analyzed appropriately and used for the right purposes. Evaluation is a discipline that applies this kind of structure and quality to the process of collecting and using data in organizations.

The literature on evaluation is extensive (Brinkerhoff, 1987; Guba & Lincoln, 1985; Patton, 1997; Shadish, Cook, & Leviton, 1990; Stake, 1995; Wholey, Hatry, & Newcomer, 2004). This literature describes methods that range in scientific rigor from controlled quasi-experimental designs, where you can determine with a certain level of probability if the outcome was due to the program or to something else, to individual diaries of anecdotes, where the evidence is the recollections of an individual. And the literature describes multiple uses of evaluation that include instrumental, conceptual, political, and imposed (Weiss, Murphy-Graham, & Birkeland, 2005). This chapter is not a review of this literature. Rather, the purpose of this chapter is to explain how nonprofits can and should use evaluation, and any of its many methods, to create a culture of learning in their own organizations.

Evaluation is the means for regularly collecting evidence that individuals, teams, and whole organizations can use to assess progress and results and learn how to learn about progress and results. In a learning culture, evaluation is built in as a normal process of organizational worklife. Evaluation should not be something done after the fact, nor only in response to funding requirements. That would be an ineffective and inefficient use of resources. Evaluation should be as customary in the life of a nonprofit as planning, budgeting, staffing, or operating programs. Without evaluation, you cannot know if your organization is making a difference that is worth the investment, and you can't know how to improve what you are doing to maximize the impact of that investment.

In summarizing a study of James Irvine Foundation grantees, Hernández and Visher (2001) wrote,

> In the end, the project's success had less to do with whether measurement systems were developed and more to do with whether the organizations were able to create a culture that valued the process of self-evaluation. The agencies needed a new mindset that embraced data as an essential tool for improvement rather than as mere paperwork required for funding. (p. 2)

Evaluation is critical for organizational learning. It is the way nonprofits learn about themselves. Without feedback from evaluation, nonprofits are just whistling in the dark, hoping they are doing the right things and doing the right things right. With evaluation, nonprofits bring the discipline of evidence-based, outcome-focused decision making to their work. Organizations that do this well will continually improve their way of designing and managing programs and services.

It is easy for nonprofits to lose sight of outcomes. They become focused on activities rather than results, delivering services rather than the intended change in people and systems. They become immersed in the day-to-day challenges of trying to meet the needs of their constituencies while struggling to find adequate resources. By practicing the discipline of evaluation, organizations stay oriented to results and to continually learning how to better achieve the results they want.

For example, a small liberal arts college received foundation funding for a 5-year community development effort. The overarching goal was an improved quality of life for all citizens in the surrounding community through access to new computer technologies. The initiative was intended to be a collaboration among college administrators and faculty, nonprofits in the community, local schools, and local government agencies. Contrary to these intentions, in the early years of the project, the college was focused almost entirely on internal development of its technology infrastructure, with community partners receiving relatively little benefit from the funding.

An evaluation process was designed to look for indicators of alignment between college and community activities and indicators of improved quality of life for everyone in the community, but especially for the underserved sectors of the community. This examination of the level of alignment and change was presented periodically to stakeholders for their interpretation over the course of the project. From this examination, stakeholders realized that early project activities would not achieve intended results.

This process of evaluative inquiry contributed to the college and community recognizing weaknesses in the project's structure and becoming realigned with their intended goals and desired outcomes. The college changed from being inward focused (installing state-of-the-art technology and teaching faculty and students how to use new technologies) to being outward focused (providing community-wide access to technology and training, linking previously underserved sectors to resources), and the community became more engaged with college resources. This created an environment in which local nonprofits and government agencies discovered how, through collaboration with each other and the college and by leveraging modest resources, they could use technology to improve the lives of their constituents. Without evaluation and its constant attention to alignment, process improvement, and results, it is unlikely the community as a whole would have benefited significantly from this project.

Evaluation has become an essential part of standards for conduct of nonprofits. The Maryland Association of Nonprofit Organizations has developed "An Ethics and Accountability Code for the Nonprofit Sector" that has become a model for the nation. In that code, "organizational evaluation" follows "mission" in importance. The designers of this code believed that evaluation is a tool for ensuring that the organization's activities are aligned with its mission. The document states, "Evaluations should be candid, be used to strengthen the effectiveness of the organization and, when necessary, be used to make programmatic changes" (Maryland Association of Nonprofit Organizations, 1998–2007).

Evaluation is

- Part science and part art: It combines social science's applied research methods with creative decisions that make the information credible and useful to various stakeholders.
- Part objectivity and part subjectivity: It combines uninvolved, third-party examination with embedded participation in the organization and judgments shaped by evaluator experience.
- Part neutrality and part advocacy: It merges the disinterested views of evaluators with their intent to use the findings to improve the lives of constituents.
- Part numbers and part stories: It combines statistics that describe the attitudes and behavior of a population with case studies and anecdotes that explain those numbers.
- Part proving and part improving: It combines accountability for results with an opportunity for the organization to improve itself. (Millett, personal communication)

Evaluation is asking questions and using the answers to improve performance and be accountable for results. It is collecting evidence of the nature and extent to which a program or organization is making progress toward and contributing to intended and un-intended results. How this information is collected and used, and how it is used for organizational learning, can vary considerably among and within organizations.

Historically, evaluation has been used to judge the worth and merit of programs. However, it is also "a set of processes that leads to individual, team, and organizational learning" (Preskill & Torres, 1999, p. xxi). In addition, it leads to community learning. It is easy in our society, with its emphasis on right and wrong, good and bad, worthy and unworthy, winning and losing, to assume that evaluation is about sitting in judgment of others' efforts and, as has often been the case, placing blame. Although, under certain circumstances, there might be good reason to substantiate the failure of an organization, learning depends on more than this. The value of evaluation for nonprofits is in building their capacity to continuously improve performance, not in sitting in judgment of individuals.

Evaluation is discovering what works, what doesn't work, and why. It is taking that information and making changes in individuals, teams, the organization as a whole, and its community. Evaluation is understanding what it is about the learning process that is helping staff improve performance and sustain that performance over time. Also, evaluation is identifying aspects of the organization that are barriers to learning and high performance.

The process of examining this information is often what helps organizations change. Self-examination is a powerful change process. Start weighing yourself frequently and regularly, and soon you will begin to lose weight. So it is with organizations. If they examine themselves regularly, they will pay attention to the things that matter and do what is necessary to improve performance.

Not all program evaluation is for the purpose of organizational learning. Often, formal evaluation in nonprofits is driven by funding requirements of a foundation or government agency. Receiving a grant may be contingent on evaluating the program being funded. The focus in these situations is accountability to the funder, not on learning. For example, a Boys and Girls Club received a grant from a foundation to start a new career development program for its youth. As a condition of receiving this grant, the club was required to submit regular evaluation reports to the funder. Staff proceeded to collect data systematically about the number of youth served; the amount of counseling, job visits, testing, and other resources that were provided to the youth; attitudes of the youth toward the program; and the staff and guardian observations about change in the youth. The findings provided a comprehensive picture of the program at a point in time.

What was missing was an evaluation of the organization's capacity to assist youth in their career development. For this Boys and Girls Club, a focus on career development of youth was a fundamental shift in its mission. Sure, it could provide grant-funded career development services. And there was plenty of evidence that they were doing that. But was it prepared to make a shift from an activities center for youth to a place that prepares youth for the world of work? The program-focused evaluation did not address these organizational alignment issues. The stakeholders, such as club staff and the national organization, had no way of knowing from the program-focused evaluation if the club had the capacity to effectively manage and sustain the new direction and, if not, what they needed to do to develop that kind of organization.

Program-focused evaluation efforts and program improvements are important, but they are not necessarily organizational learning. If the improvements are only incremental change in people and programs, without building the capacity of the organization to improve continuously, then the organization has not learned from evaluation. It is only when learning becomes pervasive in the organization that nonprofits operate more effectively and efficiently in all aspects of their work. This learning must be sustained over time. Change becomes part of the very fabric of organizational life, not just spot-cleaning the surface stains.

Developmental Evaluation

Use evaluation to look for indicators of progress toward and achievement of strategic goals. Use evaluation to understand what it is about the learning process that is helping employees and volunteers improve and sustain their performance over time. Use evaluation to identify aspects of the organization that are barriers to learning and high performance. Having and using this information is what helps organizations continuously become more effective.

Patton (2006) labels this kind of evaluation "developmental evaluation." He writes that "The evaluator is part of a team whose members collaborate to conceptualize, design and test new approaches in a long-term, on-going process of continuous improvement, adaptation, and intentional change" (p. 30).

This approach is especially important in highly dynamic organizations that are continuously changing. Evaluation has to change as the organization's mission, goals, and programs change. With these shifts in direction, the questions that an organization asks keep changing, and therefore, the evaluation focus and methods must change.

Everyone in nonprofits should be frequently asking themselves and their organizations:

- What are we doing as an organization?
- Is this what we should be doing? Are we aligned with our goals?
- How well are we doing? Are we making progress toward our goals? Are we achieving our goals?
- How can we improve what we are doing?

If no one is asking these questions, it is unlikely staff and volunteers will confront the most fundamental issues. This is not about commitment to the mission. Without a structure and process to make evaluation happen, even the most dedicated and productive staff and volunteers will not step back from "doing good" to ask themselves if this is the best way to achieve their goals (i.e., Is this what we should be doing?). This is the double-loop learning question.

Whether it is called "evaluation" or "planning" or "monitoring" or "performance measurement," it should be focused on learning. Nonprofits can apply the simplest observations or the most sophisticated scientific measurement and analysis techniques, but if they do not learn from these stories and statistics, the evaluation is a waste of time and money, and worse, staff lose respect for the methods.

There is some utility in using measurement to ensure that staff comply with expectations and standards. However, this assumes that if staff know their performance is being measured, they will do their best. This is not always the case, especially if staff don't believe in the value of what they are doing. Doing the wrong thing better does not help your customers or your organization. To continuously improve and build the capacity to continuously improve, an organization must look at itself in the mirror and ask itself double-loop questions.

The After-School Corporation of New York and Big Brothers Big Sisters discovered helpful lessons (Little, 2004) from evaluating their mentoring programs. These are useful lessons for any evaluation and have become the following principles:

1. Develop a mindset in favor of evaluation for program improvement. Promote evaluation as a tool for learning, not a means for judging and punishing.

2. Build evaluation into program design. Make it an integrated part of program development, not a separate, tangential aspect of the organization's activities.

3. Manage the data burden with staffing, expectations, and relationships. Engage staff in spreading the responsibility for data gathering so that it is not onerous and disruptive.

4. Be intentional about the logic of your program. Communicate the rationale for what the organization is doing and what the organization is trying to achieve. Use evaluation to examine the efficacy of these relationships.

5. Disseminate evaluation results strategically. Get the findings in front of people who can use the knowledge to make a difference in the organization. Do this in a way that they will be motivated to hear the results and act on the findings.

Stakeholder Focus

Start and end with the stakeholders. Be stakeholder focused. Find out what stakeholders want to learn and why, and then decide how the evaluation can be done to optimize their learning and sustain learning across the organization. An example of being stakeholder focused is a study done for American Humanics, Inc. (AH), a national organization that prepares college students for careers in the nonprofit sector. In evaluating its organization, AH listened to the questions of board members, the president, and staff. In the past, the organization had sent a questionnaire to students every few years to assess effectiveness. This provided interesting "customer" perceptions, but the survey did not answer the stakeholder questions. AH stakeholders wanted to know what made AH successful, how students used the AH experience to make the transition to working in nonprofits, and if this was the same or different in different kinds of higher education institutions. To answer these questions, four exemplary campus programs of the 70 in existence at the time were studied intensively. Individual interviews of staff and focus groups with students were conducted at each of the four institutions, in addition to reviewing archival documents. This provided case studies of four unique programs and explained how national AH works to support these very different types of programs across the country. A questionnaire survey of all students in AH programs could have provided some useful data, but it could not answer the questions being asked by the stakeholders.

It is the tendency of nonprofit leaders to make the mental leap from "we need to evaluate" to "we need a survey." When you do this, you are getting ahead of yourself. You first need to understand what you want to know about your organization and why you want to know it. Then, think about how you want to use this information, what will be credible to your audiences, and what information you already have in your files. Only then should you begin to think about the method of collecting data. Otherwise, you are putting the proverbial cart before the horse. Worse yet, you are expecting the horse to stand on its hind legs and push the cart up the hill.

To achieve learning, the design and implementation of any evaluation process should be stakeholder focused. Key stakeholders should have input into all phases of an evaluation. Staff, customers, funders, and community members all have a need to learn what works, what doesn't, and why. After all, if you want them to learn, it must be their evaluation. The design and implementation should be focused on the organization's needs, not the needs of the evaluator. In addition, too many evaluation efforts have made rigid adherence to particular research methods more important than finding the answers to questions that will help the organization be successful.

Stakeholders should be involved every step of the way. They should contribute to clarifying the mission, goals, and intended outcomes of the organization. They should be able to explain their theory of how the intended changes will occur in people and systems. They should list the questions that they want the evaluation to answer. They should help select methods and design the approach to answer these questions. The stakeholders should support the data collection process by cooperating with it and encouraging others to cooperate. They should look at an analysis of the data and offer their own interpretation and what they think are the implications of the findings. And, finally, they should create a plan for using the findings to improve organizational performance.

It's not the elegance of the design that matters; rather, it's the usefulness of the information. In fact, keep it simple (without compromising accuracy). Consider practicality as well as accuracy. The point is to collect data (numbers, descriptions, stories) that help stakeholders understand the progress that employees, volunteers, and the organization are making toward strategic goals and organizational improvement. These stakeholders need to know what is working well and what should be changed. For example, board members of a museum were sending the message, by what they said and what they supported with their donations, that they wanted noncontroversial, mainstream artists represented in the museum. Because of this, staff took fewer risks and invited a more limited range of artists; as a result, the museum was not able to expand its patron base. However, presented with evidence that their actions were a barrier to achieving the museum's goals, those trustees decided to change their behavior and support more creative programs. Interviews with staff regarding their perceptions of board member intentions were sufficient evidence. Until trustees had this feedback, they were not aware and did not understand that their influence was causing a problem for the future of the museum.

Evaluation Method

The specific design and scope of evaluation should be determined by the questions you and other stakeholders want answered. If you want to know if program X is more effective than program Y, or if program X is more effective than doing nothing at all, a controlled, quasi-experimental study is probably the best approach. This kind of study compares groups of people who, theoretically, differ only in whether they have been exposed to the program being evaluated, exposed to a different program, or exposed to no program at all. In doing so, you can rule out that any change was due to factors other than the program intervention itself.

For example, stakeholders might want to know if a new group mentoring program for young males who are without fathers in their homes contributes significantly more to self-esteem than does the current individual mentoring program. Stakeholders might want to know if it is worth the investment of dollars they are making in that new program. One way to answer these questions is to randomly assign the young males, after measuring their self-esteem, to one of three groups: (a) group mentoring, (b) individual mentoring, or (c) no mentoring. Then, after an equivalent period of time, measure their self-esteem again. If there is an increase in self-esteem in the two mentoring groups and it is significantly more for group mentoring, then you can be confident that this change was due to that particular program intervention and not to other factors.

These kinds of studies, considered the crème de la crème of evaluation, are always problematic. The costs and administration of these studies are substantial. Rarely can one be confident that different groups of people, even if randomly assigned, are truly equivalent on all factors and will have exactly the same experience save for the program intervention being evaluated. You might be able to run controlled experiments on plants in a laboratory, but when it comes to social experiments, controlling human factors and program conditions is always difficult.

Beware, also, that these narrowly focused studies of program effects do not necessarily address organizational learning. Learning questions take the form: "What do we know about serving population X?" "Should we be serving that population?" "Are we organized in the best way to serve that population effectively?" "What do we have to do differently, and what is the likely result of that change?" "Are the organization's actions aligned with intended outcomes?" Answering these questions does not require experimental studies. Much of the information needed to answer these questions might already be in the archives of the organization or can be collected through interviews with key stakeholders who have the relevant experience. Or, a panel of experts who have experience with this kind of nonprofit might provide sufficient insight. Planned observation of work processes and meeting dynamics might provide the evidence you need. The challenge is to collect data that are compelling to stakeholders given the questions that are being asked.

Findings must be credible. However, credibility is in the eye of the beholder. Find out what will be acceptable and convincing evaluation methods and evidence to key stakeholders, and gather and report data accordingly without compromising your standards for high-quality information.

Contracting with an external evaluator might be necessary, if only to bring the perception of objectivity to the findings. The general assumption is that external evaluators are independent and un-biased, but human beings are never completely unbiased. Professional evaluators bring their own values, experiences, and perceptions to the task, which is what makes them helpful.

Evaluation can also be used to ensure that desired outcomes are achieved. The process forces stakeholders to clarify their intended results. To be evaluated, the organization must be clear about how it wants to help people and organizations change for the better. Is the goal that children learn to read? Is it that families stay intact? Is it that pregnant teenagers receive prenatal care and deliver healthy babies? Is it that a river meets water quality standards for the first time in years? Is it that residents of a midwestern U.S. city enjoy a local concert of South African music and dance? By being explicit about the outcomes you want, you are more likely to achieve positive results.

It is a myth that evaluation can be done without affecting the process and outcomes of an organization. Evaluation is an organiza-tional intervention. Evaluation brings heightened attention to services and customers, it requires operational accommodation to various methods of data collection, it interrupts normal functioning of programs and activities, and it raises expectations that something will be changed as a result. As evaluation becomes integrated into the ongoing operations of your nonprofit and becomes an embedded process for organizational learning, this assumption that evaluation must have objective distance will no longer be a concern.

Success Case Method

Maybe you consider evaluation to be too costly and time consuming, and a distraction from doing your job. This mental model is the result of too many evaluation studies that are costly, time consuming, and a distraction. Evaluation does not have to be that way, nor should it be that way. Hundreds of thousands of small nonprofits do not have the resources to hire external evaluators and devote large amounts of employee time to rigorous, formal data collection and analysis. Simple, efficient, and cost-effective methods are available.

One evaluation method that fits these criteria is the Success Case Method (SCM) (Brinkerhoff, 2003). SCM is a method of evaluation that uses some of the best aspects of the more traditional methods, but does this in such a way as to be efficient, credible, and useful. When done well, it is a powerful learning and management tool.

SCM seeks to answer four basic evaluation questions about the impact of an organization and its programs:

1. What is really happening?

2. What results are being achieved?

3. What is the value of the results to customers, the organization, and the community?

4. How can the actions and organization be improved to achieve the intended results?

The purpose of SCM is to discover why some people are effective and why other people are not effective, and what can be learned from their experiences. SCM examines how the organization affects this success and failure of its staff and customers. Selected individuals who report that they have been effective because of the intervention are interviewed to discover the nature of their success and the reasons for it. In this way, you learn what is possible and what the organization must do to be successful. From this discovery, you know what to reinforce, and you know what systemic barriers need to be eliminated. The method is straightforward, is relatively easy to apply, and produces useful information very quickly.

SCM follows five basic steps:

1. Plan the study, including clarifying the purpose, stakeholders, participants, time frame, and procedures.

2. Create an impact model (see Chapter 9) to understand what is considered success for this particular organization.

3. Identify best and worst cases through a survey or other appropriate means.

4. Interview key informants and document their stories.

5. Communicate findings, conclusions, and recommendations to stakeholders.

As a result of using SCM, staff can know quickly and easily what is working and what they need to change. They can document stories of success that are interesting and informative to staff and customers. They can increase the knowledge base of the organization, provide models of successful application, and be accountable to key stakeholders.

An example of SCM is an evaluation of a training program designed to help social service providers be more effective in assisting individuals who live in poverty. Content of the training included differences in economic cultures, how those differences affect opportunities for success, how to develop an action plan to improve services to clients, and how to improve retention rates of newly hired, low-income people. Specifically, the study investigated the extent to which participants used the theories and skills from the class in their work, and to what extent the application of this learning contributed to worthwhile outcomes and results. The study also investigated organizational factors that may have mediated impact from the training. These findings were intended to be used to formulate recommendations for how to ensure that this training initiative achieved its intended results.

A brief e-mail survey was sent to the 250 individuals who attended the first training programs. Of the 75 respondents, 43% claimed to have applied their learning in ways that they believed led to concrete and worthwhile results. Four percent claimed virtually no application or value. The majority (49%) reported that they had applied at least some of their training but could not claim any concrete results. Respondents who reported the most and least success in applying learning from the program were identified. In-depth telephone interviews were conducted with 10 survey respondents who reported positive impact from the training and five who reported no impact.

From these interviews, the evaluators concluded that

• Employees with direct client contact should be a priority for this program. They were the ones most likely to apply their learning soon after the training.

- Participants should come to the training prepared. They should bring a specific issue, client, or case problem on which they want to focus during the training. They should work with their supervisors to determine an appropriate situation on which to focus. By doing this, they will begin applying their learning immediately.
- Participants should be given an opportunity to practice new skills and approaches to client services in the safe environment of the classroom, with immediate feedback from their team members, before trying the skills back on the job.

Evident from this SCM evaluation is that not only would changes in the training design enhance learning and improve performance of participants, but changes in the way the organization supervises employees and schedules training would help facilitate learning and performance. This example shows how learning at the individual, team, and whole organization levels is necessary for serving the customer.

Evaluation for the purpose of learning requires understanding not just about what happened but why it happened, and how to change the organization and system to achieve better results in the future. As Michael Quinn Patton (2003) has argued, "Evaluation is not about filling out a form for someone else, it is about not wasting time and resources on not doing good."

Accountability

When nonprofit managers talk about evaluation, they often mean holding people accountable for what they did and, incidentally, program improvement. Accountability is usually for controlling people, money, and activities so that people of influence, such as funders, have confidence that resources are being used wisely.

To put it simply, evaluations are for either control or learning. By "control" I mean using evaluation to ensure that resources are used appropriately, that a program is on schedule, and that the organization is accountable to an external funder or agency for results. By "learning" I mean using the information to build the capacity of the organization. Both control and learning are important, but organizational change depends on learning, not control.

Nonprofit leaders often emphasize accountability at the expense of learning. A study of 60 nonprofits that received grants from a private foundation supports this observation. The grantees were asked about their evaluation practices. The norm was to describe what they did with the grant money, ask participants for their immediate reactions to those programs, and summarize some descriptive statistics about outputs (i.e., number of activities and number of people who participated). Absent were meaningful discussions of outcomes and any assessment of the significance of those outcomes. Little effort was made to try to understand why these nonprofits got the outcomes they got, and what should be changed about the organization to achieve desired outcomes in the future. These nonprofits were saying to themselves, "If my funder wants us to evaluate the program, I will, but it is not what I want to do because it will take time, energy, and money away from our programs."

Evaluation for organizational learning does not necessarily require the same time and expense as studies for accountability. Those kinds of rigorous studies that are intended to meet scientific standards, and often conducted by an external evaluator, could certainly contribute useful information to the discussion about the effectiveness of an organization. However, what is important from a learning standpoint is a process that results in organization-wide self-examination and change. For that, you need continuous evaluation on a day-to-day basis by the people implementing the various programs and services of the organization. Everyone should be asking themselves questions that cause them to reflect on the quality and effectiveness of their actions—individual, team, whole organization, and community.

Evaluation in this sense is about collecting information that can be used for feedback. This is evaluation that

- examines the culture and asks: Do we have an environment that is conducive to fulfilling our mission in a way that is consistent with our values? Do we support, through incentives and recognition, the behavior that we want?
- examines work processes and asks: Are the structures and processes in place to fulfill our mission? Do we do our work in a way that will achieve the results we want?
- examines products and services, and asks: Is what we offer customers (social services, education, employment assistance, advocacy for social

justice, conservation, artistic expression, etc.) what our customers want and need? What evidence do we have? Do our products and services meet our standards for quality?

- examines employee performance and asks: Are employees committed to meeting the needs of customers? Do they have the competencies to be effective in their jobs?
- examines customer experience and asks: What do customers think about their interactions with the organization? Do they value the experience? Would they use our services again?
- examines organizational goals and asks: Are we making progress toward our goals? Is what we are doing aligned with what we want to achieve? Will these activities and processes get us to where we want to go?

These should be the frequently asked questions of your nonprofit. Meet regularly with employees, board members, volunteers, and customers, as appropriate, to ask yourselves these questions, discuss the answers, and develop solutions to problem areas.

Many nonprofits ask some of these questions on an annual basis. This might be okay for completing an annual report, but it is not adequate for learning and capacity building. Like growing a garden, evaluation for learning requires constant tending. You can ignore it for a long time, and you will still have a garden, but not the beauty and bounty that you desire. You must ask the tough questions and ask them frequently. This will cause staff and volunteers to think about what and why and how they are doing what they are doing. This will also model the questioning and reflection process that will help everyone learn how to learn.

Evaluation of American Humanics, Inc., was described earlier in this chapter. The organization undertook an evaluation to develop its capacity to gather outcomes and impact data on an ongoing basis, and use this information for organizational improvement and for communication and marketing strategies. From evaluation, much was learned about how AH affects current students, alumni, nonprofit agencies, and local colleges and universities.

Findings indicated that the total AH program, including courses, co-curricular activities, internships, and other related volunteer experiences, can have a profound impact on students, alumni, agencies, and campuses. Student attitudes, competencies, and careers are affected deeply by the AH program experience. AH students develop a commitment to the mission of nonprofits. They learn knowledge and skills that make them more effective than entry-level employees who have not been in AH. Agencies and universities are enhanced by the presence of the AH program in their communities. They benefit from the focus on nonprofit education that AH brings to the campus and community. Alumni of AH have an immediate impact on agencies and continue to make major contributions to the nonprofit sector long after they begin their nonprofit careers. Their skills and networks are valuable additions to the local agencies.

Findings from this study of four programs could not be generalized to all AH campus affiliates (i.e., assumed that the outputs and outcomes of all would be the same). But that doesn't matter. What does matter is knowing the factors that must be in place to be successful. The evaluation tells us that to the extent that these factors do exist, a program has the potential to have a similarly positive impact.

The impact study findings also suggested that AH faces challenges to developing and maintaining high-quality programs on affiliated campuses. One major challenge is ensuring that every program has a director who is a strong, active advocate for AH on campus and in the community. Another challenge is ensuring that all AH students experience a high-quality internship. A third challenge is ensuring that the passion and skills of graduates do not dissipate over time; that graduates continually develop their abilities to respond to the changing needs of the nonprofit sector.

As a result of this study, AH had impact data that could be used for organizational learning, accountability, organization development, and marketing purposes. This information was of interest to various stakeholders, such as members of the board of directors, campus/executive directors at affiliated colleges and universities, AH students, local nonprofit employers, national nonprofit partners, collaborating professional organizations, funders, and alumni. The information was also of interest to the wider higher education and nonprofit communities. Moreover, this study was just the start of an ongoing process of data collection and analysis for learning and continuous improvement by the national office of AH and affiliated programs.

The evaluation of AH is an example of how feedback and reflection in a large organization can result in learning.

Evaluation for Reflective Inquiry

An example of reflective inquiry is a 2-year evaluation of a new nonprofit educational services organization. The external consultants who conducted the evaluation identified serious challenges to the long-term sustainability of the organization, and a conventional final report was presented to the organization's board. An organization not focused on learning would have been satisfied at that point. Instead, this group wanted to use the findings to improve organizational performance, and they asked themselves four questions: What about the findings resonates with each of us? What additional questions do the findings prompt us to ask about our organization? What challenges do we face in building our organization? and What opportunities do we have to strengthen our organization? These board members were not satisfied with simply knowing; they wanted to build capacity. They asked themselves the tough questions that resulted in rich discussions of purpose, direction, and action.

When evaluation is used for reflective inquiry, when it is done regularly, when it is sown into the fabric of the organization, and when it is used for capacity building, the benefits are substantial. Organizations that use reflective inquiry well bring clarity to their goals, align their actions with their goals, are aware of how much progress they have made, have evidence of meaningful results, can communicate feedback to staff and volunteers, think about the meaning of the feedback, learn how to learn, and experience continuous improvement.

First ask the results-oriented questions, then ask the learning-oriented questions, and then ask change-oriented questions. Ask customers—employees and volunteers—some variation of these questions:

- What are the organization's goals?
- What are we doing to achieve those goals?
- What are the consequences of what we are doing?

- Is this the right thing to be doing?
- How well are we doing it?
- How can we do it better?
- Are we achieving our goals?

Next, ask the deep-dive questions:

- What have we learned that will help individuals (employees, volunteers, and customers) be successful?
- What have we learned about how teams need to work in this organization?
- What have we learned about how this organization needs to work to achieve the results we want?
- How can we use that learning to enhance our capacity to be successful?

Then ask the professional practice questions:

- What can we contribute to informing practice in this area?
- What can we contribute to the body of knowledge about this work?
- How can we contribute what we have learned to make a difference in the field?

These reflective questions should be applied to all activities, processes, and systems within the organization. Involve representatives of the key stakeholders (such as staff, customers, board members, volunteers, suppliers, community partners, and others who have a vested interest in the performance of the organization) in this reflection. They are more likely to use the results for their own learning if they are involved from the outset. Collaborate with them to decide what should be evaluated, what questions should be asked of whom, what documents should be reviewed, and how the information will be used once it is collected.

Principles of Evaluation

The following suggestions will help you make evaluation a useful process for organizational learning:

Involve staff (internal customers of evaluation) in deciding what to measure and how to measure it. Ask them what they want to know and why. Ask them for their thoughts about the data collection methods that you are recommending. Ask them to help pilot these methods to see if they will produce the information that you need. Often, a workshop format that allows these stakeholders to work together as a group is useful. This process of answering measurement questions with input from key stakeholders can be more valuable in developing a high-performance organization than the actual data that are collected.

Choose the method of measurement only after deciding what to measure. The tendency is to use a questionnaire survey to measure just about everything. But many other methods can be more useful depending on what you want to know. The appropriateness of each of these methods depends on the kind of data needed, the sources of those data, the circumstances for collecting the data, and how the data will be used. For example, you probably shouldn't send a questionnaire to users of a literacy program, and you probably shouldn't convene a focus group of users of a drug treatment program (unless meeting in that group is part of their treatment). If board members are influenced by statistics, then give them charts and graphs. If board members are influenced by client stories, then tell stories. Fit the method to the evaluation questions and learning styles of stakeholders, not the other way around. Table 8.1 gives examples of how intended outcomes are matched to a measurement method.

Collect data that are credible to stakeholders. Managers might accept the accuracy of staff interviews and focus groups, whereas board members might listen only to output (e.g., number of people served) and financial data. One group wants to hear numbers; another group wants to hear stories. Know your audience so that you can collect data and report findings that key stakeholders will find credible.

Collect and report data that are useful. The fact that clients rate the agency 4.5 on a 5-point scale or that the cost of the adult day care program has gone down 10% in the past year is not useful data for learning. The distribution of ratings across different client groups and why they rated the agency this way would be more useful to know. The reasons for the 10% drop in day care costs and the implications for improving the quality and future of the program would be useful to know. Consider what data will help stakeholders understand the organization and make critical decisions.

Table 8.1   Intended Outcomes and Measurement Methods

Intended Outcome (Examples)	*Measurement Method*
Extent of general customer (client) satisfaction	*Mailed survey:* Customers (clients) are sent a questionnaire to assess their satisfaction with products and services and their perceptions of the organization. They are asked to answer a list of questions that are mostly closed ended, using rating scales. These surveys can include several open-ended questions, but all questions must be general in nature.[a]
Extent of customer (client) satisfaction with each program and service of the organization	*Online survey:* Customers (clients) are directed to a Web site that they access with a secure password. The site guides them through a questionnaire that branches to different sets of questions according to their answers to previous questions.[a]
Qualities of the organization that affect customer (client) attitudes and behavior	*Focus groups:* Small groups of customers (clients), employees, volunteers, or community stakeholders are invited to come together to discuss the organization. This is highly structured and moderated by someone experienced in small group facilitation. Participants are asked a set of questions to assess their attitudes, beliefs, and perceptions of the nonprofit, its products, and its services. The method usually produces stories, descriptions of the nature of the customer experience, and common themes.
On-the-job behavior of staff	*Structured observation:* Using a guide with predetermined behaviors to observe, a trained observer sits in offices, meeting rooms, and activity areas and records the actions of staff, volunteers, and customers.

Intended Outcome (Examples)	Measurement Method
	Individual interviews: Ask supervisors about the performance of the people they supervise; ask staff and volunteers for stories that demonstrate application of what they have learned; ask questions that allow for confidential disclosure of the strengths, weaknesses, and ways to improve the organization.
Compliance of staff with performance standards for each service area	*Mystery (secret) shopping:* Trained auditors, acting as typical customers (clients), evaluate the programs and services of the nonprofit. They record their experience against a predetermined set of indicators. These "customers," unknown to staff, experience the nonprofit as if they are regular customers. This can be done in person, by phone, and via e-mail.
Immediate customer (client) experience of the organization and its services	*Intercept interviews:* Customers (clients) are interviewed on site, immediately after using the nonprofit's services. The experience is fresh in their minds. This method ensures that you hear from current customers and customers who are less self-selecting and biased than the typical respondents to surveys.
Knowledge of staff	*Tests:* Staff answer a set of questions (yes/no; multiple choice; short answer) that assess their knowledge about a specific topic (such as managing volunteers, fundraising, nonprofit financial management, employment law).
Fit with best practices in the field	*Panel of experts:* A small group of highly experienced nonprofit leaders provides its opinions about the quality of an organization in relation to best practices and its recommendations for change.

(Continued)

Table 8.1 (Continued)

Intended Outcome (Examples)	Measurement Method
Consensus among staff about how the organization is performing and why	*Delphi technique:* This is a type of survey in which the findings are reported back to the respondents one or more times until the respondents as a group have achieved consensus about their perceptions of the organization.
Daily events that demonstrate change in the organization	*Logs and journals:* Selected customers, staff, and volunteers are asked to record (on paper or electronically) a description of their day-to-day contacts with the organization and their reactions to those contacts.
Events that occur over time and their significance for organizational learning	*Learning histories:* Documenting the facts of an event in the life of the organization and then having key stakeholders report their reactions and actions in response to this event.
Trends in performance over time	*Archival records:* Nonprofits have planning documents, budgets, reports, audits, meeting minutes, proposals, and so on that can be used to track selected process efficiency and effectiveness indicators. For example, absentee records could be a proxy for change in employee/volunteer engagement.

a. Many good resources are available for designing and conducting surveys. This is a skill that takes knowledge and experience. Depending on the complexity and scope, consider hiring a survey expert for this task (see Salant & Dillman, 1994; Sudman & Bradburn, 1982).

Report findings in a manner in which stakeholders are receptive to the information. This has to do with the format in which information is reported. You will want all of the various stakeholders to understand your findings and be able to act on the implications. Keep it simple, relate it to the goals that are important to the particular audience, and recommend what should be done about the results. Do not just report numbers; explain what the numbers mean to the organization. Tell the story that explains the statistics.

Measure the process as well as the outcome. Continuous improvement is achieved by regular assessment of where people are in the process of achieving their goals. Adjustments to the process can be made, especially as you learn more about staff needs and the organization becomes clearer about its goals. Do not wait a year. Give yourself the opportunity for short-term adjustments that will have long-term impact.

Provide just-in-time and just-enough information. Give staff the information they need, when and where they need it. Learning is maximized when people are not overwhelmed with new information, they can relate new information to their work, and they can apply that information to a problem on the job immediately.

Measure to improve the process, not to blame or punish. Our tendency is to feel threatened by anything that might reveal a lack of personal competency. When we feel threatened, we become less cooperative and less willing to improve performance. Do everything that you can to assure participants that the measures are not being used to make judgments about individuals. Follow through on this promise. Use the data only to help individuals learn, make changes in the organization, and plan for additional activities that will make a difference in everyone's performance. Do not use the data to chastise or penalize. As Peter Drucker said, "The question isn't, Do you make mistakes? It's, Do you learn from them?" (Grant, 2002).

Knowledge Management

How can evaluation findings be managed within an organization? Simply collecting and presenting evaluation information is not enough for organizational learning. If evaluation information is not communicated among people and departments, the organization cannot make good decisions.

Hoarding and protecting information is often not intentional; it is built into the structure and culture of many nonprofits. However, the

Tool 8.1 Evaluation Planning Worksheet

This worksheet is designed to help you plan an organizational evaluation. Start with the evaluation question, identify indicators (kinds of data) that will answer that question, select an appropriate method to observe those indicators, and then create a time line for implementing each aspect of the evaluation. Examples are provided in each column.

Evaluation Questions	Indicators	Methods	Time Line
What were the reasons for creating this organization in the first place?	• Historical documents • Reported experience and observations of key stakeholders	• Review 501(c)(3) filing document • Review mission statement • Review initial proposal to funder(s) • Interview funders, board members, and staff who were employed in the beginning	By end of year

result is that much knowledge in organizations goes unshared and unused. The three deadly disasters in the NASA space program have all been attributed in part to a failure to share information among scientists and engineers at NASA and contractors to NASA. The structure and culture of NASA did not encourage and facilitate the sharing of information. If federal and local agencies had been sharing security information before the 9/11 World Trade Center disaster, they might have seen a pattern of unusual activities that posed a threat. These examples of failure in cross-functional communication are extreme, but the underlying problem is what occurs in nonprofits every day. One part of the organization has knowledge that would be more useful if shared with other parts of the organization. When this knowledge is shared appropriately and effectively, it is knowledge management; when it is not, it is knowledge mismanagement.

Perhaps you have had the experience of working on a project for several months, only to discover that a coworker down the hall from you completed a similar project 2 years before without good results. Or, the new service your organization is providing to its customers was tried before but there is no record of the development, implementation, and results. Or, you contracted out for Web design services and then found out that someone else in your organization is already working on a new Web site. Or, an employee job satisfaction survey was conducted a few months ago, and so far, there has been no discussion of the results among staff. In each of these cases, evaluation information (knowledge) was not managed effectively.

> Knowledge management is . . . a conscious strategy of getting the right knowledge to the right people at the right time and helping people share and put information into action in ways that strive to improve organizational performance. (O'Dell & Grayson, 1998, p. 6)

Knowledge management is mostly about transferring information and best practices from one part of an organization to another part. This means managing both human and technological sources of information, turning this information into knowledge, and getting it to people when and where they need it. The generic steps in the knowledge management process are to create, identify, collect, organize, share, adapt, and use internal knowledge and best practices (O'Dell

& Grayson, 1998). Effort is not wasted on reinventing the wheel and unnecessary errors. When the knowledge management process is done right, the whole organization gets smarter.

Two kinds of knowledge exist in organizations. Tacit knowledge is the informal and uncodified learning that resides primarily in the minds of employees. Explicit knowledge is formal and codified; it resides in paper documents and computer files and can be accessed by staff, assuming they know where to find this information (Nonaka, 1991).

The American Institute of Architects went through a period of self-examination that resulted in a refocus and reorganization around knowledge management. Like many professional associations, they had been focused on providing information to members rather than facilitating the exchange of information among members. They were not taking advantage of the rich knowledge base of the membership, and they were not being responsive to the way their members learn. The association decided to leverage the tacit knowledge of members and staff by creating a new structure that is intended to be more responsive to the way members use information and create knowledge (Salopek, 2004).

Knowledge management does not necessarily require sophisticated computer technology. You need only to create opportunities for staff to share both tacit and explicit knowledge with other employees and volunteers who can benefit from the information and experience. Encourage experienced staff to describe their successes and learnings from similar projects. These learnings can take the form of subjective insights, intuition, or hunches. By making all of this information explicit, others can test the validity of the conclusions.

Asking people to share information is not enough. Provide a clear vision for knowledge management in the organization. Help staff understand how knowledge management will help them achieve their strategic goals. Create incentives (they do not have to be monetary) for transferring information across departments. Provide opportunities for employees and volunteers to meet to share their experiences on similar projects and what they learned from these efforts. Show staff that nonoriginal ideas are valued. Make it easy for staff to enter project information in a database that is accessible to all. Provide resources for gathering and using the organization's information.

Do not assume that just because you have cross-functional work groups or teams that knowledge and best practices are being shared among departments. Group members have to believe that knowledge and best practice sharing are their responsibility and that it is essential to learning and to the success of the organization. Also, you have to create an environment where people feel safe in divulging what they have learned.

Training and knowledge management should be complementary (Van Buren, 1999). Training is one way of conveying the organization's knowledge to large numbers of employees and volunteers. It is an important aspect of the knowledge management system. Ask trainers to design opportunities for participants to share their experience and lessons learned. Whether it is a management development seminar or a computer software class, participants should be given an opportunity to discuss their experiences related to the topic. For example, in a project management seminar, participants should share with each other what they have learned about effective and ineffective ways to work with external resources (e.g., technology suppliers). Not only will this sharing contribute to the transfer of knowledge throughout the organization, but participants will feel better about their involvement in the seminar.

Information technology can support your knowledge management system. The computer network and organization's intranet, if you have this technology, provide a place to store and retrieve information. If you have the resources, hire a professional librarian to manage the system. They usually have the training to evaluate, store, and retrieve information and knowledge and to use the latest technology to serve the information needs of their customers. Make sure that this person has a background in reference library work and experience helping people use information databases in nonlibrary settings.

Also, rapid changes in information technology that can support knowledge management are occurring, literally, every day. I hesitate to mention the names of Web-based services because that landscape may look quite different by the time this book is published. Social networking sites such as MySpace, Facebook, and LinkedIn are becoming tools for sharing and archiving information. Nonprofits can create their own sites within these online communities. Wikis, which are collaborative Web sites, can be used for communities to develop a shared meaning around information. Weblogs, or blogs, are online diaries of a chronological entry of thoughts and comments with links to other Web sites as well as to images and sound. A nonprofit's blog could be a good way to share ideas within the organization and with the wider community.

However, the use of information technology should become a focus only after you are clear about goals, values, and barriers. New computer technology is making knowledge management cheaper and more efficient all the time. So, there is a tendency to let technology drive knowledge management rather than letting information needs drive the application of technology. This is what happens when nonprofits invest in the latest "killer ap," without first assessing what staff need to make themselves more productive (Gordon, 2005). The Internet and internal intranets are powerful tools that are revolutionizing the sharing of information. Enterprise-training software is promising to create a single database for all staff learning (Stamps, 1999). But installing state-of-the-art technology is not the answer to effective knowledge management.

In fact, although much explicit knowledge can be stored and retrieved through computer systems, tacit knowledge must be tapped in other ways. Some solutions are based in technology (intranet, online libraries, databases), and some solutions are based in human interaction. Both are essential. Explicit knowledge can be posted at a Web site, but tacit knowledge does not come into awareness until people share and discuss their thoughts and experiences with each other.

Increasing the flow of information is not difficult. The challenge is helping employees and volunteers learn how to manage and apply new knowledge. Some methods you can use are the following:

1. Formal training programs that provide new information, teach skills, and shape attitudes and beliefs.

2. Individual tutoring of staff and volunteers by experts or coworkers who have relevant experience and information.

3. Publishing, marketing, and dissemination of documents that communicate organizational knowledge in an interesting and useful way.

4. Formal presentations of information to groups and teams throughout the organization that include conversations about the meaning and application of that information to each participant's situation.

5. Coaching managers on using new knowledge to achieve their goals.

6. Being a mentor to staff (especially new employees) and guiding them through finding, evaluating, and applying information they need to do their jobs effectively.

7. Using various kinds of information technology (such as document databases, discussion databases, Internet and intranet links to experts, document exchange, performance support systems, help desks, and data analysis software) to achieve the organization's goals.

Whatever the source of evaluation findings and the resulting new knowledge, you should engage stakeholders in using the information. Tool 8.2 can help you in this process. Assuming that the stakeholders have a sense of ownership in the data, what is most important is what those data mean to them. Tool 8.2 asks stakeholders to think about the findings in relation to themselves, their work, and the organization. It frames the evaluation as a means of achieving organizational improvement.

Tool 8.2	Reflective Inquiry of Evaluation Findings
This is a tool for engaging stakeholders in the findings. Convene a group of stakeholders, ask them to read the evaluation report, give them a worksheet with these quadrants, and ask them to fill it in individually. Then discuss it as a whole group. Post what they say on a flipchart or screen in front of the group, and come to consensus on the list of answers to each question.	
What in the findings resonates for me?	What additional questions do I have about the organization?
What are opportunities for strengthening our organization that are suggested by the findings?	What challenges to the success of our organization are suggested by the findings?

Summary

Evaluation is a powerful discipline for facilitating organizational learning. Evaluation makes explicit what is known about an organization. We learn what is being done, why it is being done, and how well it is being done. Evaluation tells us about progress toward and accomplishment of organizational goals. By institutionalizing evaluation, you build your organization's capacity to learn and change. This requires moving beyond assessing staff, volunteers, and customers' immediate reactions to events, and doing more examining of the entire process that facilitates individual, small group, whole organization, and community learning. The payoff comes from using this information for continuous improvement. This payoff is leveraged by having knowledge management tools and processes in place that ensure widespread sharing of tacit as well as explicit knowledge.

9

Using Models
to Facilitate Learning

It's not what you look at that matters, it's what you see.

—Henry David Thoreau

A model is, simply, a representation of the real world. Models give us clarity about the key elements of a system and allow us to check our assumptions about how that portion of the world works. Whether it is the clay model of a new car or a computer simulation of environmental tradeoffs, models help us simplify complexity enough to be able to make decisions. Models are not the real world, and we need to continually remind ourselves of that. Social systems are much more complex, nonlinear, and chaotic than any model could possibly be.

As I explained at the beginning of this book, nonprofits need to be results oriented, and they need to build their capacity to stay that way. Using models helps to build and sustain this capacity. Models are tools that nonprofits can use for clarifying goals and keeping stakeholders focused on a shared direction; that is, where they are trying to get to, not what they have always done. They are tools for making thinking visible (Bryson, Ackermann, Eden, & Finn, 2004). They are tools for organizational learning.

This chapter describes three kinds of models that can help nonprofits learn: logic models, which are used for organizational alignment; strategy maps, which are used for strategic planning; and balanced scorecards, which are used for monitoring performance. Each is a device for facilitating organizational analysis and reflection.

Organization Logic Model

An organization logic model is a graphical representation of the alignment between what your organization believes, what it does, and its goals. Alignment is critical for nonprofits, especially when the goals are amorphous and difficult to measure, such as better health care, improved education, or economic development. Lack of alignment occurs for well-intentioned reasons. One of these reasons is that the goal is overly ambitious, such as a small nonprofit that has the goal of eliminating poverty in a local community, but has sufficient resources to manage only an emergency shelter. Or, fundraising has consumed a nonprofit's mission, such as a national advocacy organization that spends most of its budget on increasing membership. Another reason for lack of alignment is when organizational history, rather than goals, drives decisions. This happened with a youth service organization that had, for 25 years, put a substantial amount of its resources into maintaining group homes for neglected and abused teenagers, thereby separating these youth from their families for long periods at a time. This allegiance to group homes continued even in the face of a new organizational resolve to keep families intact. The organization was founded to manage group homes, and staff and board members were reluctant to give up that role.

A logic model can take many different forms. Some are goal focused, some are action focused, and some are theory focused. The point is to have something that everyone—the executive director, staff, volunteers, board members, and stakeholders in the community—can quickly understand and use to frame questions, guide information collection, and facilitate reflection.

A logic model is a performance management tool. It helps people understand what the organization is trying to achieve and why. It helps individuals understand what they must do to help the organization be successful by providing a picture of the performance goals that the organization as a whole must achieve. It indicates what needs to be assessed in order to evaluate overall organizational performance.

One type of organization logic model that has proved helpful to nonprofits has these elements: assumptions, resources, activities, outputs, outcomes, impact, goals, mission, vision, and indicators. These elements are defined in the following way:

Vision: A picture of the desired future toward which the organization is working; it might not be fully attainable.

Mission: The business of the organization; its reason for being.

Goals: Results that the organization wants to achieve for individuals, other organizations, and communities.

Impact: Fundamental, long-term changes in an organization, community, social systems, or policies.

Outcomes: Specific changes in individual, team, and organization behavior; knowledge; status; and level of functioning. These can be intended or unintended.

Outputs: Direct services and products of the organization's activities.

Activities: Processes, events, tools, and technology that make up the day-to-day work of the organization.

Resources (a.k.a. "inputs"): human (including competencies, skills, knowledge, and expertise); financial; physical; and community resources that an organization has available for achieving its goals.

Assumptions: Beliefs we have about the social, economic, and political world in which we live; our community; and the work that we do that are shaping decisions we are making about our organization.

Indicators: Measurable approximations of movement toward intended outcomes and impact.

These elements are arranged in a sequential order on a chart according to the logic of the system. An example of this arrangement is a logic model that was developed for a new management support organization (MSO) in a medium-sized, metropolitan community (see Figure 9.1). This MSO used this logic model, developed early in its formation, to clarify its mission and align its operations with its goals.

Vision
Enhanced quality of life in greater metropolitan area

Mission
Helping nonprofit organizations in metro area achieve their missions through effective management.

Assumptions

- Nonprofits play a key role in quality of life
- Nonprofits will be more effective with better leadership, management, and governance
- Nonprofits will use the services of the center to improve themselves

Environments

- Funders demanding greater accountability of local nonprofits
- Strong interest in community assessment
- Attention to community indicators

Resources

- Center has endowment
- Center has experienced, capable staff
- Funders are interested in nonprofit capacity building

Activities

- Board training
- Consulting with nonprofit leaders
- Resource center for nonprofits
  - o Information and referral
  - o Technical assistance
  - o Library
  - o Demonstration projects
  - o Business planning
  - o Web site
- Professional development of nonprofit staff
  - o Training programs
  - o Annual conference/special events
  - o Peer exchange

Outcomes and Impact

- Improved board/CEO relationships
- More and better teamwork in nonprofits
- Better financial management in nonprofits
- Alignment of each nonprofit's activities with its mission

Goals

- MSO is full-service, capacity-building organization that can be replicated in other communities
- Better management by professional staff, board members, and volunteers in region's nonprofits
- Enhanced organizational effectiveness of region's nonprofits
- Goals of nonprofits are achieved

Indicators

Strategic plan complete for three nonprofits	Twenty board members have received basic board training that improved their skills as board members	Staff from 125 nonprofits have received training that helped them achieve their missions
Business plans complete for six nonprofits	Sixty nonprofits have received information and/or referrals to services or consultants that help them achieve their missions	Ten nonprofit executives have improved their leadership skills through peer exchange services

Figure 9.1   MSO Logic Model

As you can see from this logic model, alignment is not often clear-cut. For example, this organization had to ask itself, "Is a board training program what is needed to achieve improved board and CEO relationships, more and better teamwork, better financial management, and internal alignment of nonprofits in the community?" If not, "What else should we be doing to achieve these outcomes, or do we want different outcomes?" These are the kinds of questions that should be asked about each element of the model. The process of asking and answering these questions helps an organization identify priorities and apply resources to the things that are most important. Learning how to do this will give your organization useful planning and management know-how.

Logic models are developed in one direction and read in the opposite direction. To develop a logic model, start at the end (usually on the right). Prepare a chart of the elements you want in your model. Put goals on the right and inputs on the left. Then engage stakeholders in filling in the boxes. Try to sequence the information so that you move from right to left. However, be open to inserting the information as it comes up in discussion and wherever it belongs in the model.

To develop a logic model, use a series of "if-then" statements going right to left:

If these are our goals, then we need these outcomes and impact.

If these are the outcomes and impact we want, then these are the activities we need to be doing.

If these are the activities we need to be doing, then these are the resources and inputs we need.

To read a logic model, go from left to right, using a series of "if-then" statements:

If we have access to these resources, then we can perform these activities.

If we perform these activities, then we will have these outputs.

If we have these outputs, then we will achieve these outcomes.

If we achieve these outcomes, then we will achieve this impact.

If we achieve this impact, then we will achieve our goals.

The value of a logic model is not in its elegance or even its initial accuracy. The value is in the process of groups of staff and board members working on creating, validating, and modifying the model. In these conversations, participants become aware of what they want the organization to become, what they are doing and not doing to get there, and what will be needed in order to be successful. This should be an iterative process of continually checking assumptions and making changes in elements of the model (W. K. Kellogg Foundation, 1998, 2004).

This same process can be used at every level of the organization. A project team working on preschool programs can take stock of how well what it is doing is aligned with the youth development goals of the organization as a whole. A project team working on a major musical event can take stock of how well what it is doing is aligned with the music education efforts of the performing arts organization.

A small, private foundation used this process of developing a logic model as a way to create a shared vision for its future. By bringing the five staff members together and engaging them in a conversation about the content of the model, staff were able to go to their board united around their purpose and direction. Their logic model continued to evolve over time. An early version of the model is shown in Figure 9.2.

Creating a logic model with your staff and board is not only an opportunity to bring clarity and shared commitment to mission and action, it also tells you how to evaluate your organization. At the macro level, you can compare the model to what currently exists. The gaps become apparent, and you can decide if your organization should change or the model should change.

At the micro level, the model tells you what needs to be measured as part of an overall evaluation. For example, in the model for the private foundation, we see that participation of low-income people in decisions about their communities is a major indicator of their success. Many foundations, in practice, make distribution of funds the primary indicator of success. This particular foundation was saying that "payout" is not enough; it wanted to see evidence of more empowered leadership in the target communities. This was a significant learning for the program officers in this foundation. As a result of the process of creating a logic model, they could go to their board and explain the logic of what they were doing and why it was important.

In summary, the benefits of using a logic model are the following:

- You have a common understanding of what you are doing and where you are going as an organization; getting everyone on the same page.

Vision A classless, borderless world in which each child has equal opportunity to achieve/succeed and in which all people can participate in public decision making.

Mission To increase opportunity for low-income people and communities in the metro area, especially by directly supporting efforts to enable people to participate effectively in public life.

Values and Beliefs

1. We believe there is wisdom in the people; we value participation by low-income people as a moral imperative and because it effectively produces results.
2. Family and community are fundamental; we value institutions that build their political power.
3. We believe we should be a "wedge" foundation, the "first in" on important issues, a risk taker that seeks leverage.

Environment

1. Climate of opinions and political systems is indifferent to low-income people.
2. Organizations serving low-income people believe foundations are inaccessible.
3. Moment of opportunity for us given leadership chanes in city.

Resources

- Money
- An informed board
- Staff who are seasoned practitioners
- Access to public, civic, and philanthropic leaders
- Diversity of staff and board
- Great grantees
- A reputation of integrity, innovation, and responsiveness

Activities

- Be transparently clear about our goals and priorities; communicate them actively.
- Be highly accessible.
- Connect individuals and organizations to build capacity, change policy and politics, and leverage our grant investments.
- Scan information appropriate to our grantmaking decisions; know what's out there.

Outcomes and Impact

I. Outcomes
  A. New/increased interventions—organizing methods, technology use, advocacy models, institutions—to ready and involve low-income people in
    1. community decision making
    2. public policy development
    3. political processes
  B. New/changed agendas for action in any of these three areas as products of the involvement of low-income people.
  C. More low-income people becoming
    1. community organizers
    2. public policy advocates/analysts
    3. elected or appointed officials
  D. More/stronger community organizations and policy advocacy organizations in which low-income people have leadership roles
  E. More useful action research describing and evaluating all of the above
  F. More philanthropies investing more resources in issues, people, organizations we have "jump started"

Goals

1. More inclusive community decision making, public policy development, and political processes and institutions that fully involve low-income people in decisions that affect their lives
2. Increased economic, social justice, political, and educational opportunities for low-income people
3. Increased access by organizations of low-income people to philanthropic resources, political tables, and policy-making circles
4. A pace-setting, bridge-building foundation that contributes knowledge to practices of achieving the above

Increased number and effectiveness of organizations of low-income people

Complete and communicated revisions of grantmaking niche/strategy

Greater number of low-income people at decision-making tables via our work

Greater number of readable, useful documents describing/ evaluating effective participatory interventions

Increased number of proposals funded in this niche

Increase in number of changes to policy and practice made with involvement of low-income people

Figure 9.2   Private Foundation Logic Model

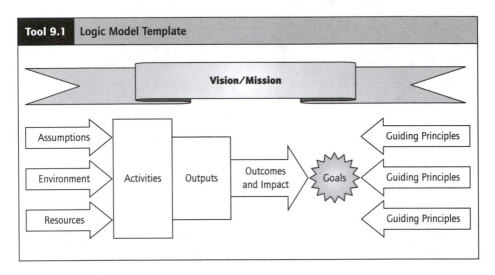

Tool 9.1   Logic Model Template

- You identify gaps in the logic—stakeholders saying such things as "We're not clear about that"; "That's not achievable"; "That's not our mission"; "We're not doing anything to get that outcome."
- You put the focus on performance and results, not just activities.

Organizations have difficulty being clear and explicit about what they believe they do that actually brings about change in their customers. Nonprofit organizations tend to be so focused on action that they lose sight of how that action will help them achieve their goals. When this happens, we see a lack of alignment between actions and goals. And this results in inefficiencies, wasted resources, and poor performance.

The logic model template (see Tool 9.1) is a tool for helping organizations examine their theory of change and compare this theory to what is actually happening in practice. They can decide what must change in order to achieve alignment. What is it that the organization believes will lead to success? How does it intend to have an impact on people, institutions, and systems? Does it have the right goals but the wrong actions, or the right actions but the wrong goals? Or, are both goals and actions a poor fit with the mission of the organization?

Here are some options for using this template to develop a logic model for your organization.

Option 1—Convene your leadership team. Using the template, facilitate a discussion to fill in the model's elements. Start with brainstorming elements that would go into each box. Then, look for congruity and alignment among boxes. Compare this to what team members believe is the current reality of how they function. Ask, "What should change, and how should we change it?"

Option 2—Analyze the organization using interviews, focus groups, observation, and existing documents, and then create a model that you think best represents the current reality. Present it to the key stakeholders for validation and modification. Discuss the gaps between current reality and how they want your organization to bring about change.

Option 3—Form a small team of key stakeholders. Ask them to create a logic model for the current reality of the organization. Have them present it to the larger stakeholder group. Discuss how close this is to what they believe is their theory of change. What are the gaps, and what are the implications of having those gaps?

Use the worksheet in Tool 9.2 to work with your organization on creating a logic model.

The elements of the model that is created from this worksheet become the foci for evaluation and reflective inquiry. Are we doing what we said we would do? How well are we doing it? How are we doing on our indicators of success? Are we getting the outcomes that we wanted? If not, why not? Are we achieving our goals? If not, why not? These are the questions for reflection.

Strategy Map

Strategy maps, a special kind of logic model, are for long-range planning. Often, they begin with brainstorming that leads to an affinity map, which results in a causal map (Bryson et al., 2004). These models work well when a new organization is forming. Stakeholders can be brought together to brainstorm what they know about the environment, potential resources, shared assumptions, purposes, goals, and strategies. Often, at this point, strategies become confused with goals, and clarity around the differences becomes critical. For example, stakeholders in a newly forming middle school reform organization struggled with their mission. Should it be to develop a comprehensive program that results in middle schools having better outcomes for kids, or should it be to develop a statewide network of schools engaged in middle school reform? Mapping out their strategy helped to make this dilemma clear to them. A logic model framework (see Tools 9.1 and 9.2) can help in the development of a strategy map.

Tool 9.2 Organization Logic Model Worksheet

Resources	Activities	Outputs	Outcomes	Impact	Goals
What resources do staff and volunteers need in order to perform the activities?	*What programs and services do we need to provide in order to achieve desired outcomes?*	*How much activity and how many people do we need to serve to achieve intended outcomes?*	*What changes in individuals, teams, the organization as a whole, and the community do we want?*	*What changes in institutions and systems do we want?*	*What results do we want for our customers/clients?*

Balanced Scorecard

Another model that can help in evaluation and learning in nonprofits is the balanced scorecard. The balanced scorecard tool, sometimes called a dashboard (Oakes, 2004), is a chart of a selected set of indicators of organizational performance, typically including indicators of mission, financial health, stakeholder satisfaction, infrastructure capacity, and process efficiency. Made popular by Kaplan and Norton in the business sector, the usefulness of this tool has been demonstrated in nonprofit organizations with much success (Chang & Morgan, 2000; Kaplan & Norton, 2001; Niven, 2002).

Much of the value of the nonprofit scorecard is in the process that nonprofits must go through in selecting outcomes to measure, identifying indicators of progress toward those outcomes, and observing effects of changes that are made to maximize organizational results. The scorecard is just the locus of energy for a process of evaluation and organizational learning that involves critical decisions about what is important to measure and what should be done about the results. This process can be a powerful learning experience for nonprofits.

After much discussion, the staff and board members of an urban hospice decided that the best indicator of their financial performance was the number of filled beds. They could have used total revenue, cost savings, amount of donations, or a number of other typical indicators of financial performance, but they decided that filled beds was the best single indicator given their goals as an organization. So, they decided to periodically post that number on a chart that all employees and volunteers could see. Board members looked at it to get a quick read on how well the organization was doing financially. To increase the number of filled beds, staff started to pay attention to such things as wider marketing of the agency to hospitals and clinics in the area, staff training, and staff retention. Just that one measure provided this nonprofit with a motivating assessment of where they were and what they needed to do to improve. More importantly, they went through a process of staff and board members deciding together what was the best indicator given their mission and goals.

Tool 9.3 presents options from which you can select indicators to track your organization's performance. Select one or two key indicators in each of the five areas and track these over time. Display the

Tool 9.3	Nonprofit Balanced Scorecard Menu of Indicators

Financial Health

- Balanced budget
- Cashflow
- Administrative costs/program costs
- Revenue diversification
- Donations
- Endowment
- Long-term funding
- Value of assets

Mission

Outputs

- Number of people served
- Number served from target populations
- Programs offered

Outcomes

- Community safety
- Access to education
- Healthy people
- Healthy environment
- Efficient/safe transportation
- Affordable housing
- Community involvement
- Growing/sustainable economy
- Diverse cultural opportunities

Stakeholder Satisfaction

- Client satisfaction
- Staff satisfaction
- Board of trustees satisfaction
- Community perception
- Repeat use of services by clients
- Staff turnover

Process Efficiency

- Staff response time
- Time client served by agency
- Cost of service
- Cost of service per client
- Quality of response to client
- Office appearance
- Task completed when promised

Infrastructure Capacity

- Knowledge/skills of staff
- Staff-to-client ratio
- Strategic plan
- Policies aligned with mission
- Information technology aligned with mission
- Physical resources aligned with mission

data regularly on a single chart so that staff can see at a glance how they are doing and where they need to target their continuous improvement efforts.

The balanced scorecard makes performance measures explicit and understandable for everyone. It makes performance transparent and gives all employees clear targets toward which they can work.

The balanced scorecard is about systemic change, helping staff make the shift from a focus on projects and programs to continuously looking at the organization as a whole. By taking a balanced approach that tracks indicators of total organizational functioning, the scorecard facilitates learning for sustained success over the long term. It is not only about a balanced budget or how many clients were served; it is also about such things as meeting the needs of clients, creating a supportive workplace, securing the necessary resources, and providing products and services efficiently.

Selection of indicators for a balanced scorecard can be assisted by a strategy map. What is it that the nonprofit believes will lead to success? How does it intend to have an impact on people, institutions, and systems? Once you and other stakeholders identify these various elements of your organization's impact, then "scorecard" indicators can be addressed. What can be observed about the organization that will indicate progress toward and attainment of goals? What will indicate financial health? What will indicate stakeholder satisfaction? What will indicate an effective infrastructure? What will indicate efficient processes? And, most important, what will indicate that the mission of the nonprofit is being fulfilled?

The process for creating and implementing a balanced scorecard typically follows five phases:

1. Confirm the organization's vision, mission, goals, outcomes, outputs, activities/work processes, and context. What is the organization trying to accomplish, and how does it want to do this?

2. Develop consensus around several indicators for each of the five areas of performance: mission, financial health, stakeholder satisfaction, infrastructure capacity, and process efficiency. Decide on targets for each of these indicators.

3. Design a chart that displays the indicators for each of the areas of performance and track these indicators over time (e.g., line graph).

4. Train staff and board members in using and maintaining their scorecard.

5. Formulate an ongoing implementation plan that explains how the organization intends to maintain or improve these indicators.

6. Monitor and evaluate change in indicators over time.

Summary

Models of organizational systems can be powerful tools for learning. The logic model, strategy map, and balanced scorecard, and the process of creating and maintaining these tools, facilitates learning about what needs to be done to maximize organizational performance. By using these tools, staff will learn what is truly important to them to achieve. They will learn how to use evaluation data to monitor and improve performance. They will have learned to use a process and tools that will help them continue to improve performance in the future. Like an architect's drawings for a new building, these tools present a simplified and manageable view of what you and your staff are trying to build together.

10

Summary

Demand for effectiveness is coming from many constituencies. Politicians, local communities, board members, volunteers, and employee groups are all putting pressure on nonprofits to fulfill their missions, and to do so in a responsible and cost-effective manner.

If nonprofits are to be effective over the long term, they must create a culture of learning. And to create a culture of learning, they must constantly be evaluating themselves and using this information to improve performance and achieve results. This is the central message of this book.

This book has explained how nonprofits learn and how that learning occurs through a process of feedback and reflection. Incremental enhancement of knowledge and skills from training and education programs is important to learning, but these instructor-led, individually focused programs are only a small part of what must happen. The kind of learning needed for organizational success comes from individuals, teams, whole organizations, and communities learning together and learning how to learn together.

The focus must be on creating a *culture of learning* within the organization and in its relationship with its wider community. A culture of learning contributes to continual organizational improvement. A culture of learning is an environment that supports and encourages evaluation and the collective discovery, sharing, and application of knowledge. In this kind of culture, employees and volunteers are continuously applying collective knowledge to problems and needs. To create a culture in which learning is the rule, not the exception, nonprofits must remove the barriers to learning and reward risk taking, action learning, reflection, and feedback.

Creating and maintaining a learning culture requires regular assessment of the culture and then using that feedback to adjust and change. Nonprofits must take the time to step back, take a look at themselves, make sure that what they are doing is aligned with what they want to achieve, and then have the courage to change if needed.

In a nonprofit culture of learning, four levels of learning are happening simultaneously: individual learning, team learning, whole organization learning, and community learning. Evaluation facilitates learning at each of these levels.

Individual Learning

All organizational learning starts with individuals. However, to improve capacity of the organization, this learning must become collective. Individuals can learn in organizations in a way that contributes to organizational effectiveness, not just personal development. Individual learning provides the building blocks for team, whole organization, and community learning.

Team Learning

When managed well, teams make better decisions and are more productive than individuals. Organizational learning can contribute to the development of well-functioning teams. To build these teams, nonprofits must bring people together who want to achieve the same goals, share their knowledge, support each other, work collaboratively, and share the recognition and rewards of their success. Most importantly, they must learn together and learn how to learn as a team.

Whole Organization Learning

Whole organizations can learn and learn how to learn collectively from evaluation. Whether a three-person advocacy group or a 1,000-employee international relief organization, success depends on learning being a collective activity. Whole organizations can learn how to manage knowledge and how to make decisions and solve problems as an enterprise. This learning builds the capacity of a nonprofit to deal with challenges to sustainability, such as a changing environment, shifts in resources, new accountability pressures from stakeholders, and demands for evidence of significant impact.

Community Learning

Nonprofits have an obligation to serve their communities. However, the definition of a nonprofit's community is broad. It can be defined by geography, membership, or constituency. Regardless of the kind of community, nonprofits should help their communities use evaluation to create a culture of learning that will help the participants in those communities achieve their goals. Nonprofits can develop a relationship with their communities built on continuously learning together and learning how to learn together.

Learning From Evaluation

Organizational evaluation is critical for learning and creating a culture of learning. It is the way nonprofits find out about themselves. Evaluation is the process of collecting and interpreting data about progress and performance and using that information for feedback and reflection.

Learning how to do useful evaluation is learning how to learn. An organization that can do this well will be able to continually improve its way of designing new programs and how it manages itself for continuous performance improvement. The discipline of evaluation is a learning process. When done well, it puts the focus on results and on learning how to achieve results. Nonprofits that are constantly evaluating their programs and their organization and using that information in strategic planning are going a long way toward creating a culture of learning.

Evaluation generates a great deal of information. This knowledge must be managed effectively if it is to have value for continuous improvement. Managers need to understand the use of knowledge management technology; however, they also need to understand how to help others manage and apply organizational knowledge that is not recorded in a computer database. Managers need to help employees and volunteers make this knowledge explicit and available to everyone.

Learning From Models

Logic models and balanced scorecards can be very useful tools for learning. Their regular application contributes to a culture of learning. A logic model shows the alignment, or lack of alignment, between the intended outcomes of the nonprofit and how it spends its time and energy. A balanced scorecard helps monitor and sustain alignment over time. However, the primary value of either of these types of models is in the discussion and solutions that emerge from identifying their elements.

Getting Started

Make a commitment to creating and supporting a culture of learning. Convene your key internal and external stakeholders, and use that meeting to map out your organization. Look for gaps in alignment and decide how to change so that actions are aligned with mission. Put in place mechanisms for evaluation and feedback about individuals, teams, the whole organization, and your relationships with your community. Provide opportunities for everyone throughout the organization and community stakeholders to reflect on that feedback and develop consensus on solutions. Repeat this process periodically. Attend to and nurture a culture of learning over time.

One tool you can use to help you get started is the Organizational Learning Maturity Scale (Tool 10.1) to see where your nonprofit stands in terms of developing a culture of learning. The scale has two dimensions. The first is the focus of learning. Does the organization primarily care about methods used for delivering instruction, or the learning outcomes of training and development programs, or learning for achieving the strategic goals of the organization, or learning for building capacity, or creating a learning culture? Nonprofits may

Tool 10.1	Organizational Learning Maturity Scale					
		Stage of Learning Maturity				
Level	Method-Focused Learning	Outcomes-Focused Learning	Strategy-Focused Learning	Capacity-Focused Learning	Culture-Focused Learning
Individual	Training and development programs are topical and off the shelf.	Learning activities are for the purpose of developing knowledge, skills, and attitudes needed to achieve results in the individual's workplace; training is customized and delivered when needed.	Learning activities are designed to help individuals achieve the strategic goals of the organization.	Individuals have learning plans; learning activities encourage feedback and reflection; action learning is applied often; knowledge is shared among individuals; individual beliefs and values are addressed.	Expectations for ongoing learning are made clear to new employees and volunteers; information is shared freely among employees and volunteers; every employee and volunteer has a learning plan; individual learning is recognized and rewarded.
Team	Team training, if it happens at all, is generic; the team goal is to complete the assigned task.	Teams evaluate themselves on the basis of intended outcomes achieved; teams seek to learn why they did or did not achieve intended outcomes; teams try to improve performance.	Teams understand the vision and mission of the organization; teams are continually evaluating themselves on the basis of achieving organizational goals; teams try to learn from experience.	Teams have learning plans; teams receive tailored training in teamwork; teams assess their own effectiveness as a team and try to improve teamwork and work processes; teams regularly collect and use feedback from customers and other stakeholders.	Teams apply action learning; teams continually assess performance and use this information to improve; teams share knowledge with other teams; teams make learning one of their goals.

(Continued)

Tool 10.1 (Continued)

Level	Stage of Learning Maturity				
	Method-Focused Learning	Outcomes-Focused Learning	Strategy-Focused Learning	Capacity-Focused Learning	Culture-Focused Learning
Whole organization	There are no learning activities at this level.	Accumulated outcomes of the organization are assessed and reported.	Groups of internal and external stakeholders review performance in relation to strategic goals.	Employees and volunteers share a vision for the direction of the organization; systems are in place for sharing knowledge; collecting and learning from feedback is recognized and rewarded.	Learning is an explicit goal of the organization; knowledge management system facilitates sharing of information among individuals and teams; knowledge is readily shared across departments; physical space is conducive to learning among individuals and teams; underlying values related to actions are continually examined.
Community	There are no learning activities at this level.	Employees learn how to conduct a community needs assessment.	Employees learn how to work with community members to set goals and develop a strategy to achieve goals.	Employees and community members establish a system for continually assessing needs, establishing goals, and assessing outcomes; there is regular community feedback and reflection.	The organization has a dynamic learning relationship with the community; the organization and community are continually learning about the assets of the community and how these can be used to improve quality of life; knowledge is freely shared among the organization and the community stakeholders; the organization helps the community learn how to learn about itself.

move progressively through all of these stages, they might jump among these stages, or they might fixate on one of the stages. Many nonprofits will find that they are stuck in the method or outcomes stages. This awareness can help them take the next step.

The second dimension of this scale is level of learning. Is learning occurring at the individual level, the team level, the whole organization level, or the community level? A truly mature organization will have learning occurring at all of these levels and be focused on creating a learning culture that has the capacity to grow, adapt, and be effective over time.

Involve staff and volunteers in this organizational self-assessment. Ask them to say where in the intersections of stages and levels they think your nonprofit best fits. Where would they like it to be? What do they think the organization needs to do to get there? What does each of them need to do? The answers to these questions and the conversation about the answers to these questions will take you a long way toward intentionally creating a learning culture in your organization.

References

Adkins, B., & Stewart, C. (2004, July). Shift organizational culture to improve organizational performance. Retrieved from: http://www.exinfm .com/workshop_files/shift_organizat_culture_to.pdf

American Society of Interior Designers. (1998). *Productive workplaces: How design increases productivity: Expert insights* [White Paper]. Washington, DC: Author.

Argyris, C. (1977, Sept.-Oct.). Double loop learning in organizations. *Harvard Business Review,* pp. 115–125.

Argyris, C. (1990). *Overcoming organizational defenses.* Boston: Allyn & Bacon.

Argyris, C. (1991, May-June). Teaching smart people how to learn. *Harvard Business Review,* pp. 5–15.

Argyris, C. (1994, Jul.-Aug.). Good communication that blocks learning. *Harvard Business Review,* pp. 77–85.

Argyris, C., & Schön, D. A. (1974). *Theory in practice: Increasing professional effectiveness.* San Francisco: Jossey-Bass.

Ashkenas, R. N., Ulrich, D., Jick, T., & Kerr, S. (1995). *The boundaryless organization: Breaking the chains of organizational structure.* San Francisco: Jossey-Bass.

Axelrod, E. M., & Axelrod, R. H. (1999). The Conference Model. In P. Holman & T. Devane (Eds.), The change handbook (pp. 263–278). San Francisco: Berrett-Koehler.

Bellanet. (2002, July). An interview with Bruno Laporte and Ron Kim. Retrieved from: http://www.km4dev.org/index.php?module=uploads& func=download&fileId=60

Best practices. (2004, Mar.). *Training,* p. 62.

Bohm, D. (1996). *On dialogue.* New York: Routledge.

Bradley, B., Jansen, P., & Silverman, L. (2003, May). The nonprofit sector's $100 billion opportunity. *Harvard Business Review,* pp. 94–103.

Brinkerhoff, R. O. (1987). *Achieving results from training: How to evaluate human resource development to strengthen programs and increase impact.* San Francisco: Jossey-Bass.

Brinkerhoff, R. O. (2003). *The success case method: Find out quickly what's working and what's not.* San Francisco: Berrett-Koehler.

Brinkerhoff, R. O., & Gill, S. J. (1994). *The learning alliance: Systems thinking in human resource development.* San Francisco: Jossey-Bass.

Brown, J. (2001). The World Café: Living knowledge through conversations that matter. *Systems Thinker, 12*(5). Retrieved from: http://www .theworldcafe.com/articles/STCoverStory.pdf

Bryson, J. M., Ackermann, F., Eden, C., & Finn, C. B. (2004). *Visible thinking: Unlocking causal mapping for practical business results.* New York: Wiley.

Carnevale, A. P., & Gainer, L. J. (1989). *The learning enterprise.* Alexandria, VA: American Society for Training and Development and U. S. Department of Labor.

Carver, J. (2006). *Boards that make a difference: A new design for leadership in nonprofit and public organizations* (3rd ed.). San Francisco: Jossey-Bass.

Catsambas, T. T., & Webb, L. D. (2003). Using appreciative inquiry to guide an evaluation of the International Women's Media Foundation Africa program. *New Directions for Evaluation, 2003*(100), 41–51.

Chang, R. Y., & Morgan, M. W. (2000). *Performance scorecards: Measuring the right things in the real world.* San Francisco: Jossey-Bass.

Chronicle of Philanthropy. (2008, Jun. 10). IRS says number of charities rose 6% in 2007. Retrieved from: http://philanthropy.com/news/government/ index.php?id=4917

Cooperrider, D. L., Sorensen, P. F., Jr., Whitney, D., & Yaeger, T. F. (Eds.). (2000). *Appreciative inquiry: Rethinking human organization toward a positive theory of change.* Champaign, IL: Stipes.

Cory, D., & Bradley, R. (1998). Partnership coaching. *Systems Thinker, 9*(4), 1–5.

Dannemiller, K. D., James, S. L., & Tolchinsky, P. D. (1999). Whole-scale change. In P. Holman & T. Devane (Eds.), *The change handbook* (pp. 203–216). San Francisco: Berrett-Koehler.

Daudelin, M. W., & Hall, D. T. (1997, Dec.). Using reflection to leverage learning. *Training & Development,* pp. 13–14.

Drexler, A., Sibbet, D., & Forrester, R. (1988). The Team Performance Model. In W. B. Reddy & K. Jamison (Eds.), *Team building: Blueprints for productivity and satisfaction.* Alexandria, VA: NTL Institute; San Diego, CA: University Associates.

Drucker, P. F. (1996). Foreword. In F. Hesselbein, M. Goldsmith, & R. Beckhard (Eds.), The leader of the future: *New visions, strategies, and practices for the next era.* San Francisco: Jossey-Bass.

Fahmy, D. (2007, Dec.). Everybody wants to save the world. *Inc. Magazine.* Retrieved from: http://www.inc.com/magazine/20071201/everybody-wants-to-save-the-world.html

Frydman, B., Wilson, I., & Wyer, J. (2000). *Organizational learning: An explorer's guide.* San Francisco: Butterworth-Heinemann.

Gallwey, T. (2000). *The inner game of work.* New York: Random House.

Garvin, D. A. (1993, Jul.-Aug.). Building a learning organization. Harvard Business Review, pp. 78–79.

Gery, G. J. (1991). *Electronic performance support systems.* Boston: Weingarten.

Gerzon, M. (2006). Leading through conflict: How successful leaders transform differences into opportunities. Boston: Harvard Business School Press.

Gill, S. J. (2000). *The manager's pocket guide to organizational development.* Amherst, MA: HRD Press.

Gilley, J. W., Boughton, N. W., & Maycunich, A. (1999). *The performance challenge.* Reading, MA: Perseus.

Goleman, D. (1998, Nov.-Dec.). What makes a leader? *Harvard Business Review,* pp. 93–102.

Gordon, J. (2005, Aug.). Making knowledge management work. *Training,* pp. 16–21.

Grant, E. A. (2002, Sept.). The uber mentor. *Inc.* Retrieved from: http://www.inc.com/magazine/20020901/24536.html

Grant, H. M., & Crutchfield, L. R. (2007, Fall). Creating high-impact non-profits. *Stanford Social Innovation Review.* Retrieved from: http://www.ssireview.org/articles/entry/creating_high_impact_nonprofits/

Guba, E., & Lincoln, Y. (1985). *Naturalistic inquiry.* Beverly Hills, CA: Sage.

Hammonds, K. (2003, May). Investing in social change. *Fast Company.* Retrieved from: http://www.fastcompany.com/magazine/71/socialcapital. html

Harvey, J. B. (1996). *The Abilene Paradox and other meditations on management* (2nd ed.). San Francisco: Jossey-Bass.

Healy, K., & Hampshire, A. (2002). Social capital: A useful concept for social work? *Australian Social Work, 55*(3), 227–238.

Hequet, M. (1993, Feb.). The limits of benchmarking. *Training,* pp. 36–41.

Hernández, G., & Visher, M. G. (2001). *Creating a culture of inquiry: Changing methods—and minds—on the use of evaluation in nonprofit organizations* [Report]. San Francisco: James Irvine Foundation.

How are we doing? (2000, Fall). *Philanthropy Matters, 10*(2), 6–7.

Isaacs, W. (1999). *Dialogue: The art of thinking together.* New York: Doubleday.

Jacobs, R. L., & Jones, M. J. (1995). *Structured on-the-job training.* San Francisco: Berrett-Koehler.

Kaplan, R. S., & Norton, D. P. (2001). *The strategy-focused organization.* Boston: Harvard Business School Press.

Katzenbach, J. R., & Smith, D. K. (1993). *The wisdom of teams: Creating the high-performance organization.* Boston: Harvard Business School Press.

Kim, D. H. (1993a). The leader with the "beginner's mind." *Healthcare Forum Journal, 36*(4), 32–37.

Kim, D. H. (1993b). The link between individual and organizational learning. *Sloan Management Review, 35*(1), 37–50.

Kleiner, A., & Roth, G. (1997, Sept.-Oct.). How to make experience your company's best teacher. *Harvard Business Review,* pp. 172–177.

Kretzmann, J. P., & McKnight, J. L. (1993). *Building communities from the inside out: A path toward finding and mobilizing a community's assets.* Evanston, IL: Northwestern University, The Asset-Based Community Development Institute, Institute for Policy Research.

Light, M. (2001). *The strategic board: The step-by-step guide to high-impact governance.* New York: Wiley.

Light, P. (2000). *Making nonprofits work: A report on the tides of nonprofit management reform.* Washington, DC: The Brookings Institution Press.

Lippitt, L. L. (1998). *Preferred futuring: Envision the future you want and unleash the energy to get there.* San Francisco: Berrett-Koehler.

Little, P. M. D. (2004). Learning from organizations that learn. *Evaluation Exchange, 10*(1), 14–15.

Losada, M. (1999). The complex dynamics of high performance teams. *Mathematical and Computer Modelling, 30*(9-10), 179–192.

Marquardt, M. J. (1996). *Building the learning organization.* New York: McGraw-Hill.

Maryland Association of Nonprofit Organizations. (1998–2007). *Standards for excellence: An ethics and accountability code for the nonprofit sector.* Retrieved from: www.marylandnonprofits.org/html/standards/04_02.asp

McCambridge, R. (2006, Spring). Research and nonprofit excellence. *Nonprofit Quarterly,* pp. 11–17.

McKinsey & Company. (2001). *Effective capacity building in nonprofit organizations* [Report]. New York: Author.

National Civic League. (1999). *Civic index: Measuring your community's civic health* (2nd ed.). Denver, CO: Author.

National Civic League. (2001). *Community building in Kansas City: Lessons learned* [Report]. Denver, CO: Author.

Niven, P. R. (2002). *Balanced scorecard step-by-step: Maximizing performance and maintaining results*. New York: Wiley.

Noer, D. M. (1996). *Breaking free: A prescription for personal and organizational change*. San Francisco: Jossey-Bass.

Nonaka, I. (1991, Nov.-Dec.). The knowledge-creating company. *Harvard Business Review,* pp. 96–104.

Oakes, K. (2004, Jul.). A dashboard for learning. *Training & Development,* pp. 20–22.

O'Dell, C., & Grayson, C. J. (1998). *If only we knew what we know.* New York: Free Press.

O'Mara, M. A. (1999). *Strategy and place.* New York: Free Press.

O'Neill, M. (2002). *Nonprofit nation: A new look at the third America.* San Francisco: Jossey-Bass.

Oregon Progress Board. (2003). *Is Oregon making progress? The 2003 benchmark performance report.* Retrieved from: http://www.oregon.gov/DAS/OPB/docs/2003report/Report/2003BPR.pdf

Oregon Progress Board. (2007). *Breakthrough results for Oregon: Revamping Oregon's approach to a sustainable future.* Retrieved from: http://www.oregon.gov/DAS/OPB/docs/OSIII/OSIII_Concept.doc

Osborne, D., & Plastrik, P. (2000). *The reinventor's fieldbook: Tools for transforming your government.* San Francisco: Jossey-Bass.

Overholt, A. (2003, Aug.). Charitable deductions. *Fast Company.* Retrieved from: http://www.fastcompany.com/magazine/73/socialcapital.html

Owen, H. (1997). *Open space technology: A user's guide* (2nd ed.). San Francisco: Berrett-Koehler.

Patton, M. Q. (1997). *Utilization-focused evaluation: The new century text* (3rd ed.). Thousand Oaks, CA: Sage.

Patton, M. Q. (2003, May 19). Presentation to Michigan Grantmakers-Grantseekers 2003 Conference, Lansing.

Patton, M. Q. (2006, Spring). Evaluation for the way we work. *Nonprofit Quarterly,* pp. 28–33.

Pearn, M., Mulrooney, C., & Payne, T. (1998). *Ending the blame culture.* Aldershot, UK: Gower.

Peters, T. (1992). *Liberation management.* New York: Fawcett.

Pfeiffer, J. W. (Ed.). (1989). *The encyclopedia of group activities: 150 practical designs for successful facilitating.* San Diego, CA: University Associates.

Porter, M. E., & Kramer, M. R. (1999, Nov.-Dec.). Philanthropy's new agenda: Creating value. *Harvard Business Review,* pp. 121–130.

Porto, K. (n.d.). Encouraging corporate cultural shift using the World Café. Retrieved from: http://www.theworldcafe.com/stories/fpa.htm

Preskill, H. (2008). Evaluation's second act: A spotlight on learning. *American Journal of Evaluation, 29*(2), 127–138.

Preskill, H., & Torres, R. T. (1999). *Evaluative inquiry for learning in organizations*. Thousand Oaks, CA: Sage.

Renz, D. O. (2004). Exploring the puzzle of board design: What's your type? *Nonprofit Quarterly, 11*(4), 52–54.

Richey, R. (1986). *The theoretical and conceptual bases of instructional design*. New York: Nichols.

Robèrt, K.-H. (1997). *The Natural Step: A framework for achieving sustainability in our organizations* [Booklet]. Waltham, MA: Pegasus Communications.

Rogge, M. E. (1998). Toxic risk, community resilience, and social justice in Chattanooga, Tennessee. In M. D. Hoff (Ed.), *Sustainable community development* (pp. 105–122). Boca Raton, FL: Lewis.

Rubin, H. (1998, Fall). The new merchants of light. *Leader to Leader*, pp. 34–40.

Rummler, G. A., & Brache, A. P. (1990). *Improving performance: How to manage the white space on the organization chart*. San Francisco: Jossey-Bass.

Russ-Eft, D., Preskill, H., & Sleezer, C. (1997). *Human resource development review*. Thousand Oaks, CA: Sage.

Saguaro Seminar. (2001). Social Capital Community Benchmark Survey. Retrieved from: http://www.hks.harvard.edu/saguaro/communitysurvey

Salamon, L. M. (1992). *America's nonprofit sector: A primer*. New York: The Foundation Center.

Salant, P., & Dillman, D. A. (1994). *How to conduct your own survey*. New York: Wiley.

Salopek, J. J. (2004, Dec.). Turning member smarts into organizational wisdom. *Executive Update*. Retrieved from: http://www.asaecenter.org/PublicationsResources/EUArticle.cfm?ItemNumber=11528

Saposnick, K. (2003). A continuous learning approach to child welfare. *Systems Thinker, 14*(4), 9–10.

Schein, E. H. (1985). *Organizational culture and leadership*. San Francisco: Jossey-Bass.

Schoemaker, P. J. H., & Gunther, R. E. (2006, June). The wisdom of deliberate mistakes. *Harvard Business Review*, pp. 108–115, 146.

Schön, D. A. (1983). *The reflective practitioner: How professionals think in action*. New York: Basic Books.

Senge, P. (1990). *The fifth discipline: The art and practice of the learning organization*. New York: Doubleday.

Senge, P., Kleiner, A., Roberts, C., Ross, R. B., & Smith, B. J. (1994). *The fifth discipline fieldbook*. New York: Doubleday/Currency.

Shadish, W. R., Cook, T. D., & Leviton, L. C. (1990). *Foundations of program evaluation*. Newbury Park, CA: Sage.

Stake, R. E. (1995). *The art of case study research*. Thousand Oaks, CA: Sage.

Stamps, D. (1999, Jan.). Enterprise training: This changes everything. *Training,* pp. 41–48.

Stephens, J., & Ottaway, D. B. (2003, May 5). How a bid to save a species came to grief. *The Washington Post,* p. A1.

Sudman, S., & Bradburn, N. M. (1982). *Asking questions*. San Francisco: Jossey-Bass.

Sussman, C. (2003). Making change: How to build adaptive capacity. *Nonprofit Quarterly, 10*(4), 19–24.

Tobin, D. R. (1998). *Knowledge-enabled organization*. New York: AMACOM.

Tough, P. (2004, June 20). The Harlem Project. *The New York Times Magazine,* p. 44.

Tropman, J. E. (2003). *Making meetings work: Achieving high quality group decisions* (2nd ed.). Thousand Oaks, CA: Sage.

Tugend, A. (2007, Nov. 24). The many errors in thinking about mistakes. Retrieved from: http://www.nytimes.com/2007/11/24/business/24shortcuts.html

Vaill, P. B. (1996). *Learning as a way of being*. San Francisco: Jossey-Bass.

Van Buren, M. E. (1999, May). A yardstick for knowledge management. *Training & Development,* pp. 71–78.

Weisbord, M. R. (1987). *Productive workplaces: Organizing and managing for dignity, meaning, and community*. San Francisco: Jossey-Bass.

Weiss, C. H., Murphy-Graham, E., & Birkeland, S. (2005). An alternate route to policy influence: How evaluations affect D.A.R.E. *American Journal of Evaluation, 26*(1), 12–30.

Wenger, E. (n.d.). Communities of practice: A brief introduction. Retrieved from: http://www.ewenger.com/theory/index.htm

Wholey, J. S., Hatry, H. P., & Newcomer, K. E. (Eds.). (2004). *Handbook of practical program evaluation* (2nd ed.). San Francisco: Jossey-Bass.

W.K. Kellogg Foundation. (1998). *W.K. Kellogg Foundation evaluation handbook*. Battle Creek, MI: Author.

W.K. Kellogg Foundation. (2004). *W.K. Kellogg Foundation logic model development guide*. Battle Creek, MI: Author.

Yankelovich, D. (1999). *The magic of dialogue: Transforming conflict into cooperation*. New York: Simon & Schuster.

Zemke, R. (1999, June). Don't fix that company. *Training,* pp. 26–33.

Index

About the Author

Stephen J. Gill is an independent consultant specializing in organizational learning. He conducts organizational analyses and assesses the impact of performance improvement interventions. He is affiliated with The Learning Alliance, Inc., and the Advantage Performance Group, and his clients have included major corporations, government agencies, nonprofits, philanthropic foundations, and professional associations.

He was on the faculty of the University of Wisconsin–Milwaukee College of Education and then the School of Education at the University of Michigan. After leaving the university, he joined Formative Evaluation Research Associates in Ann Arbor as a senior consultant and became a principal and part owner of this consulting group. Next, he joined United Training Services, Inc., in Southfield, Michigan, as an executive consultant and formed an independent consulting business in 1993.

Dr. Gill earned a B.A. degree (1969) in psychology from the University of Minnesota. He earned his M.A. degree (1974) in counselor education and his Ph.D. (1976) in counseling psychology from Northwestern University.

Dr. Gill has written more than 40 articles and book chapters and developed manuals and handbooks on needs analysis, program evaluation, and human resource development. He is a coauthor (with Robert O. Brinkerhoff) of *The Learning Alliance: Systems Thinking in Human Resource Development*, published by Jossey-Bass in 1994, and author of *The Manager's Pocket Guide to Organizational Learning*, published by HRD Press in 2000. He writes the blog www.ThePerformanceImprovementBlog.com.

Dr. Gill is an elected trustee of Washtenaw Community College, Ann Arbor, Michigan. His term will end in 2010.

Supporting researchers for more than 40 years

Research methods have always been at the core of SAGE's publishing program. Founder Sara Miller McCune published SAGE's first methods book, *Public Policy Evaluation*, in 1970. Soon after, she launched the *Quantitative Applications in the Social Sciences* series—affectionately known as the "little green books."

Always at the forefront of developing and supporting new approaches in methods, SAGE published early groundbreaking texts and journals in the fields of qualitative methods and evaluation.

Today, more than 40 years and two million little green books later, SAGE continues to push the boundaries with a growing list of more than 1,200 research methods books, journals, and reference works across the social, behavioral, and health sciences. Its imprints—Pine Forge Press, home of innovative textbooks in sociology, and Corwin, publisher of PreK–12 resources for teachers and administrators—broaden SAGE's range of offerings in methods. SAGE further extended its impact in 2008 when it acquired CQ Press and its best-selling and highly respected political science research methods list.

From qualitative, quantitative, and mixed methods to evaluation, SAGE is the essential resource for academics and practitioners looking for the latest methods by leading scholars.

For more information, visit **www.sagepub.com**.